ONE IN ONE HUNDRED
LIVING WITH BIPOLAR

LORNA MURBY

WITH CONTRIBUTIONS FROM
PETER SMART & LYDIA CHAJECKI

authorHOUSE®

AuthorHouse™ UK
1663 Liberty Drive
Bloomington, IN 47403 USA
www.authorhouse.co.uk
Phone: UK TFN: 0800 0148641 (Toll Free inside the UK)
UK Local: (02) 0369 56322 (+44 20 3695 6322 from outside the UK)

Published by AuthorHouse 11/30/2021

ISBN: 978-1-6655-9514-8 (sc)
ISBN: 978-1-6655-9515-5 (e)

Print information available on the last page.

Any people depicted in stock imagery provided by Getty Images are models, and such images are being used for illustrative purposes only. Certain stock imagery © Getty Images.

This book is printed on acid-free paper.

CONTENTS

PART FOUR

FOREWORD BY PETER, LORNA'S HUSBAND

Lorna Smart(nee Murby) my late wife began this book in 2011 as a follow up to her first book "Snappy But Happy," and goes deeper into understanding Bipolar Disorder, how to live with it and what you can do to help yourself. Lorna spent many months and years happily researching and writing this book (even though she would recall her own unpleasant experiences), because she was so pleased to have moved forward and wanted to share what she had learnt to help other people.

After the writing we both spent years typing this book but unfortunately our computer crashed and we couldn't afford to have it replaced, so the project stalled. Fortunately we had saved most of the book on a memory stick.

The book itself is divided into four parts - Part 1 is Lorna's self help book; Part 2 Poems written by Lorna and myself Part 3 Short Stories by the family; Part 4 The Epilogue written by myself and Lorna's daughter Lydia about Lorna's passing. Lorna had wanted to include poetry written by the family(some dealing with Mental Health matters) and some of our short stories.

Then in early 2020 Lorna was diagnosed with primary tongue cancer with secondary tumours in her mouth and neck. Unfortunately her operation was cancelled due to the high incidence of the Covid 19 infection in Leicester(at the time the worst affected city in the United Kingdom). During a second course of radiotherapy, with a weakened immune system, Lorna caught a chest infection and passed away suddenly on 26 June 2020 - the worst day of my entire life. She was 49 years old.

In March 2021 Authorhouse got in touch to see how the book was progressing, so I told them what had happened and that we still wanted the book published. I had started my State Pension in 2020 and bought a new laptop to replace the crashed computer.

Lydia and I earnestly wanted to publish this book because there is so much of Lorna in it and also Lorna had wanted it published to help others.

This book is dedicated to Lorna's memory.

PART ONE

CHAPTER 1

INTRODUCTION

2011, is this the start of a new beginning? A new start because of my marriage to my third husband Pete on December 11th 2010. I have never been so happy. I'm feeling more confident and content than I've ever been in my life. My daughter Lydia is 12 and very pretty.

Since my first book Snappy but Happy, I have improved tremendously with my Bipolar Disorder, even when I write, I run off into a tangent. I am a person in my own little world.

Although I get periods in my life when it gets tough and I can't function properly, as a result from lack of sleep. Sometimes I can function properly and lead a normal life. You can read about my story in my first book Snappy but Happy which is available locally in Coalville, Leicestershire at Hermitage 99.2 fm on Hotel Street or at Authorhouse.co.uk.

The book Snappy but Happy is basically a true story about four women (which includes myself) who have struggled and suffered with depression and got over it. I am still battling with this terrible illness, however I'm getting there.

Each day is a challenge and is difficult for me. Some people who suffer from this illness don't have many good days but just experience bad days.

I am more positive and confident about everyday life whereas when I was down I was really negative. When I got sick in December 1999 I was more or less in a hopeless state, however this is nobodys' fault, and it's just a freak of nature.

My husband Pete is very loving, caring and patient with me. He helps me when things get tough. He makes me really happy. We got married on December 11th 2010. We have now been married 2 yr 3mths.

I don't have many manic episodes now, only when I sing, I get very elated, high and I can't seem to come down to earth. Apart from suffering from depression, I also suffer from panic attacks mainly when I go out, which isn't very often. My G.P has prescribed me Propranolol which seems to suit me. I carry this tablet wherever I go.

My husband says I'm not getting out enough and that's why I'm suffering from Agoraphobia. I'm sure if I can conquer Agoraphobia, I can conquer Bipolar (manic depression) and the panic attacks which I regularly experience especially in bed and outside the home.

Bipolar (depression) can affect anyone despite age groups, also men as well as women, teenagers or sometimes young children. This book is designed to help people of all walks of life come to terms with their depression and it is also a self-help book too. In my book 1 in 100 Living with Bipolar, there are also experiences of people who have suffered but are now on the mend.

Some people believe that life appeared by chance rather than by a creator. Other people argue that there isn't a God. Some people believe that there is a God but often blame him for all the disasters in the world. However, Revelation 4v11 states " that God is worthy to receive the glory, honour and power because he created all things and because of his will they existed and were created".

However no matter what people may think we were designed by a loving creator and we were given the ability to think for ourselves, to distinguish between right and wrong. We all have what is called a conscience and sometimes when we do wrong things in life we need to relieve that conscience by prayer. Everybody on this planet is unique in themselves. We are human beings, not programmed like robots.

Some people who live with Bipolar feel at times that they are super-human and can do almost anything. For someone who has Bipolar, manic, clinical or S.A.D (seasonal affective disorder) can experience accelerated performance in doing new things, the mind tends to absorb things more quickly than if someone was normal.

In the future maybe man will be able to self-diagnose his own illness, just as if he were visiting a doctor.

In my research of Bipolar or clinical depression, I have come across famous people and professors, very learned and highly educated people who also have Bipolar. They say that Some of the brainiest people are those that suffer from depression. In my first book Snappy but Happy (revised edition) it mainly dealt with people who suffer from Bipolar Disorder. This illness isn't an easy one to live with. From personal experience, it can be a harrowing time for both the sufferer and family members who don't fully understand the illness.

For some people who are suffering from a manic episode, they feel like they can do absolutely anything that nothing is impossible whereas, for someone who is experiencing a low period in their life, they can experience feelings of sadness or worthlessness which results in feeling like a nothingness state. You can also feel crushed (a bit like a grape) that is trodden down and had the juice zapped out of it.

Sometimes a person that is in a negative mood has feelings like giving up on life, believe me, suicide isn't the answer. We will talk about that in another chapter of the book. A depressed person sometimes feels like slow-moving traffic, not getting anywhere. This illness isn't an easy one to live with however with medical help you can achieve anything. Next, we will discuss what Bipolar and S.A.D are?

CHAPTER 2

WHAT IS BIPOLAR DISORDER AND WHAT IS S.A.D?

In my book Snappy but Happy, I concentrated on what the illness is (a form of manic depression) which stems from a chemical imbalance in the brain. Someone who suffers from Bipolar can experience mood swings, up one minute down the next, a bit like a rollercoaster at the fair. For some people that experience Mania there are moments in their lives when they have calmness and stability. Some people experience hallucinations or hear things that most people can't hear or see. It can be very frightening to the person that is suffering.

Many people that are Manic can feel elated or high when they are around people. For someone who is suffering from depression and on a high it can result as a sign of Euphoria, it's like things happen too quickly, you wish you could reverse speed just like a tape recorder.

Almost everyone suffers from mood swings, however, for someone who suffers from Bipolar, things can become more extreme in the sense they become out of control.

Referring back to my book Snappy but Happy Bipolar Disorder can affect people in different ways. Some people experience severe mood swings, up one minute down the next. When someone is low or depressive they can experience feelings of depression and despair, like being in a dark tunnel with no light in sight. When someone is high or in a manic state, they experience feelings of extreme happiness and elation. Although I am much happier within myself, I am not happy with my weight. It could be better. I've decided to go on a diet and to do plenty of exercise, this should do the trick.

When I'm depressed or on a low period in my life, I would burst into tears quite often for no apparent reason whereas when I'm on a high or in a Manic state I would laugh uncontrollably for no apparent reason. When I do this my husband says "Stop tittering" in a Frankie Howard voice.

Bipolar Disorder isn't a widely known illness amongst the general public who may only be aware of it through certain celebrities who are reported to have Bipolar such as Stephen Fry, Katherine Zeta-Jones, Frank Bruno and many others.

Bipolar Disorder (manic depression) can have its drawbacks, you can experience The following symptoms such as:

YOU CAN EXPERIENCE:

1) Poor lack of sleep
2) Lack of personal hygiene
3) Lack of concentration
4) You feel important
5) Have racing thoughts
6) Feeling high (Euphoric sensations)
7) Irritability
8) Restlessness
9) Increased sexual drive 10)Spending too much money
10) Lacking in judgement
11) You can also experience aggressive or risky behaviour, doing silly things like crossing the road without looking both ways etc. Sometimes when someone is Manic they don't realise the consequences of their actions.

Sometimes people suffer from hypomania which means a milder form of Mania, a condition which is marked by over-excitability. When someone is Manic they are at their most creative and I can only write properly when I am Manic, like lots of other creative people.

Sometimes I get really obsessed with my writing, I try too hard, I do too much, my thoughts race round my brain like a chainsaw, cutting my ideas in half with only half of my thoughts being written down in time, the other half evaporate into nothingness which ends up with me totally stressed out. I can only think of writing, sometimes I don't sleep and must write until the early morning, finishing what I set out to do.

Many doctors or psychiatrists seem to think that Bipolar runs in the family that it is a genetic problem. However, this isn't always the case because my condition wasn't the result of a genetic problem. My depression shortly began after the birth of my daughter. It wasn't her fault, it happens to women sometimes. The doctors thought I'd got Post-natal depression because I wasn't paying much attention to her so she was taken away from me. When she had been taken from me, I yearned for her to be with me. However some time later I found that the doctors had misdiagnosed me, I didn't have post-natal depression, I had Bipolar Disorder which is another name for Manic depression. This stems from an abnormality in the brain, so we are told.

It is unusual for a person to first experience symptoms of Bipolar when they are in their mid-40s'. It usually occurs when someone is in their teenage years or starts when someone is in their 20s'. In fact, most age groups can be affected by this illness. At least one person in six may suffer from depression at some point in their lives. At least 1 in 20 is severely or clinically depressed.

In order to recover from your illness, you need to learn how to manage it, to be in control. This book is designed to help you step by step on the road to recovery, it is designed to help sufferers and their families understand Bipolar and are better equipped to help.

My idea of writing this book came from personal experience and from other peoples' experiences which you can read about in my first book Snappy but Happy revised edition.

People who suffer from this illness need to find ways of coping; we will discuss this later on.

Mood swings are biologically controlled by the brains' chemistry. In a Bipolar patient when someone is significantly it causes one to become erratic in behaviour, this behaviour can result from a chemical imbalance in the brains' activity. Why this occurs we do not know, neither do scientists really, it's a bit of a mystery. Some scientists have achieved Remarkable cures for things like the common cold or a simple headache.

In fact, at present, there is no known cure for Bipolar. It's just that some people who have this debilitating illness do eventually get better. I find from personal experience popping pills seems to alleviate my Bipolar so that I'm more stable in body and mind. Although I sometimes feel like I'm rattling and rolling because of the amount of tablets I have to take each day to keep me well.

The only person who understands illnesses is the one who designed us in the first place, our creator; it's only he who knows the answer to all problems.

Referring back to my first book Snappy but Happy Bipolar can affect people in different ways. Some people experience severe mood swings, up one minute down the next.

When someone is low or depressive they can experience feelings of depression and despair whereas when someone is high they experience feelings of extreme happiness and elation. Although I am happy within myself I don't feel Manic very often now. I am more composed like a musical instrument. When I was depressed on a low, I used to burst into tears for no apparent reason, whereas when I was Manic and high I would laugh uncontrollably for no apparent reason.

It has been reported in certain newspapers that certain celebrities have Bipolar too and artistic and creative people have been known to have had Bipolar Disorder such as:

It is a known fact that Jean-Pierre Falret described Bipolar as being another word for Melancholia; this was in the year 1851.

Robert Schumann, born 1810 and lived until 1856, was a composer of German and Romantic school. He was a creative genius in his time.

Impressionist Vincent Van Gogh, born in 1853 and died in 1890 also lived with depression. Unfortunately, although he was treated for Bipolar he couldn't cope so he committed suicide.

Winston Churchill, born in 1874 and died in 1964, became a wartime British prime minister, in 1940 at the age of 66, he suffered from a form of depression (Melancholia)

which he called "Black Dog". He was also awarded the Nobel Prize for literature for his history of the English Speaking Peoples. He was also an enthusiastic artist too.

Ludwig Van Beethoven, born 1770 and died in 1827, was a brilliant pianist and composer, he never married. There were periods in his life when he was very creative and some parts of his life where he was in sheer desperation and suffered from alcoholism. Many experts speculated that he had Bipolar. There were periods in his life when he couldn't eat when he was Manic. Gradually he became deaf. During his lifetime he composed some of the greatest works such as: the oratorio, Mount of Olives, the opera Fidelio and the Pastoral and Eroica symphonies.

The singer Adam Ant, born in 1954 is also known to have had Bipolar. He was sectioned for about six months. He made a documentary in 2003 called" The madness of prince charming".

Frank Bruno, a former boxer, born in 1961, was diagnosed as having Bipolar in 2003. He was sectioned for 28 days.

Stephen Fry actor, comedian and writer born in 1957 was diagnosed as having Cyclothymia which is a form of Bipolar. He made a two-part TV documentary called The secret life of the Manic depressive. Stephen Fry said "It is infuriating. I know but I do get a huge buzz out of the Manic side. Bipolar has tormented me all my life with the deepest of depressions while giving me the energy and creativity that perhaps has made my career. I rely on it to give my life a sense of adventure and I think about most of the good about me has developed as a result of my mood swings".

Carrie Fisher born in 1957 is known for her role as princess Laia in the Star Wars films. She was diagnosed as having Bipolar at the age of 24 in 1981.

Kerry Katona born in 1980 pop singer and TV reality star suffers from Bipolar Disorder. She said "I'm an up and down person. I feel lonely and I'm afraid to go out at times." In public, Kerry said," You'll never see me down in public; I'm always bright and bubbly.

Patricia Cornwall born in 1956 a crime fiction writer was in a deep depression in her teenage years and she said, "It's not unusual for Bipolar people to have artistic talents."

Vivean Leigh, born in 1913 and died in 1967, a famous actress, had Bipolar for the best part of her life. Her second husband Lawrence Olivier noticed that his wife had symptoms which related to Bipolar. She experienced several high moments and low moments where she had a mental breakdown.

Spike Miligan, born 1918 died 2002, experienced Bipolar. He was a writer and comedian. He was best known for 'The Goon show and his wicked sense of humour. He suffered from Bipolar for most of his life. He had a lot of mental breakdowns which lasted for a year or so. He said," It's like a storm at sea, you don't know how long it will last or whether you are going to survive it." He created the TV series Q5 Q6 -9tv comedy. He was the past patron of the Manic depressive fellowship. He also appeared as himself in a cameo role 'Taking Over The Asylum'.

Irish singer Sinead O'Connor born in 1966, has been known to have had Bipolar. She had disturbing thoughts of suicide, and she got sick after the birth of her son Shaun. She was diagnosed 5mths after the birth of her son.

Sylvia Plath, born in 1932 and died 1963, was an American poet and author. She admitted that periods of her life were periods of joy, happiness and positivity and periods of despair and negativity, she said, "It's as if my life were magically run by two electric currents."
At the age of just 30yrs, she committed suicide by putting her head in the oven and turning the gas on. She was given a posthumous diagnosis of Bipolar.

Tony Slatery born 1959. In the 1990's he suffered from a mid-life crisis. He said" I used to hire an empty warehouse by the river Thames. I just stayed there on my own, didn't answer the phone or open the mail for months and months. I was in a pool of despair and suffered from mania." Tony was diagnosed with Bipolar in 1996.

Kurt Cobain, born 1967 and died 1994, was a lead guitarist and songwriter of the group Nirvana. As a child, he was diagnosed with A.D.D (attention deficit disorder). He was later diagnosed with Bipolar Disorder, he also suffered from insomnia, he also complained of stomach complaints so he self-medicated on drugs and ended up committing suicide at just 27.

These are just a few people described as having had Bipolar in their lives. When I write my thoughts on paper I often run off onto a tangent and have to continue writing my thoughts down throughout the night.

In order to accomplish my task sometimes, this takes me until the early hours of the morning to finish what I set out to do. This is when I'm at my most creative and I can only write properly when I'm manic, like lots of creative people.

Amazingly 1 in 100 people suffer from Bipolar at some point in their lives. However, the general public are not aware of this. According to doctors and psychiatrists, there are two types of Bipolar 1 and Bipolar 2. Bipolar 1 means that someone has experienced one or more episodes in their lifetime, speaking too fast, spending too much money (uncontrollably) and staying up all night are also symptoms of Bipolar 1.

Bipolar 2 is when someone has experiences of Hypomania, more than one episode of depression but with no mania.

Looking back I am more Bipolar 1 than 2 because I used to spend too much money uncontrollably whereas now I'm trying to save money for a rainy day. I am more in control of my money and my moods.

Depression isn't an illness you can see with the naked eye, it's a mental condition which affects judgement and behaviour in people that are clinically depressed. I know this from personal experience. Lots of things can cause a mental health problem, the most common being depression which can make you feel low or sad. It can affect your mood, sleep patterns and physical well-being as well It can make you physically and mentally sick.

Anxiety is one of the most causes of mental illnesses and it can affect your sleep, you can develop a racing heart, experience stomach upsets and have panic attacks which we'll talk about later.

Now we will talk about O.C.D. What is O.C.D?

O.C.D is another word for Obsessive Compulsive Disorder which affects people in 2 different ways:

1) unpleasant thoughts which keep recurring to the mind for e.g. worrying about some appliance, like the oven hob that hasn't been switched off.

2) Compulsions – keep checking and checking things to get them done.

A mental health problem can become a phobia which can cause panic attacks upon the victim i.e. spiders terrify me and so does thunder and lightning.

Bipolar Disorder is a mental health problem which is associated with experiences in mood swings lows or highs. In my personal experience of Bipolar, I have discovered the new me, I try to eat more healthily now and try to exercise each week. Usually, I go to the gym with my husband Pete and we exercise in a small group. Developing a rich healthier lifestyle doesn't happen overnight, it takes a lot of hard work and effort but well worth the rewards

It's not just famous people that suffer from depression, it's ordinary folk like me and you. This illness can be a heavy burden to carry at times, however, be positive and you can achieve anything

Sometimes when I'm ill I feel so whacked that my energy drains from my body and I feel like it's an effort to survive, so I focus on one day at a time. It's a constant battle to keep well. Remember to take your MEDICATION as this will keep you well and in control of your life. Sometimes people that are manic devote a lot of time to interests or hobbies. Rather than overdo things you need to take time out for yourself, to look after your body.

As my weight is a constant threat to my physical health, I am trying to diet and exercise so that I gradually lose weight which at present is affecting my back.

People who eat healthy foods and exercise are more likely to lose weight than people who eat rubbish and don't exercise. Many people suffer from Bipolar in different ways.

When someone is depressed they can get very emotional in different ways, a person can feel very unhappy and constantly burst into tears for no apparent reason, you can get into a can't be bothered mood and get very restless, agitated and lose your self-confidence. This is what happened to me. I lost my confidence in cookery and going outdoors. I am now getting the help I need. Sometimes when someone loses their confidence you can experience feelings of inadequacy, feelings of worthlessness and have experiences of hopelessness whereas when you are manic and on the go, you are like a cat on hot bricks. I found this to be true. When I was down I experienced feelings of hopelessness and despair with no hope in sight.

Someone who is depressed and manic sometimes experiences frequent episodes of mania and some people can't cope and resort to suicide, believe me, that is not the answer. Just imagine how your family and friends would feel if you did this.

Someone who is depressed or who suffers from mania often finds it difficult to concentrate on one thing at a time. I found this to be true with myself. I lacked concentration quite frequently. I blame the E.C.T; I was given in hospital (electroconvulsive therapy) which isn't used so much now. It can produce short or long term memory loss. I ended up losing my memory long term right to this day. E.C.T is when someone is caused to have a fit which jolts the body into a convulsion. It was supposed to make me better. However, it made me worse.

I was on a mood stabilizer called Lithium for quite a few years; however, I soon became toxic and had to come off the tablet. I now take these tablets which keep me well:

Quetiapine 300mg Depakote 250mg Zopiclone 7.5mg Chlorpromazine 25mg

Everyone is different, so my tablets wouldn't suit every individual.

A person that has depression doesn't think in a clear state of mind. Many people find in their lives that they make wrong choices which they later regret, however, if this is the case with you don't despair, don't look at the bad choices you've made, look at what you can achieve now. Don't dwell on negative emotions or your thinking may be dulled. There are also many physical things which can affect a person with depression such as:

1) constant tiredness
2) staying up all night
3) staying in bed all day
4) poor hygiene .

I had these problems at least two years ago. I had lots of problems with people name calling me at work. Another problem was a loss of appetite, however with me it was the opposite, and I put on weight.

I still find it difficult to complete one task at a time. I'm on the go twenty-four-seven, doing too many things and not completing my tasks one at a time. However, in time things will gradually get better.

I have found just lately that I talk too much, I have many plans and ideas so now and again I spend money recklessly without thinking about the consequences. When I was severely manic about two years ago I spent money uncontrollably. Now I'm married to Pete he tries to help me to be more in control of my money and not waste it, although now and again I still get the urge to spend. I know day by day that my mental health is improving as a result of my continuing to take the medication. This stops me from relapse and from feeling hopeless. By now you should know what Bipolar Disorder is

Next, we will discuss what S.A.D is:

What is S.A.D? This term means Seasonal Affective Disorder which affects some people during different seasons of the year. Some people feel down in the winter months and manic in the summer months. Approximately 1 in 50 people suffer from S.A.D. I display periods of extreme mania in the summer months and in the winter months I spend a lot of time in bed, it's as though I don't want to face the world and my Agoraphobia makes things worse. In the summer months, I have bags of energy just like a candy bar.

People that suffer from S.A.D experience these problems due to a lack of light:

Both the light and darkness cycle determines when we get to sleep and when we rise from sleep. The effect light can have on a person can determine our appetite, sexual drive, sleep patterns and our moods.

If you suffer from some of the following symptoms you may have S.A.D:

1) Alcohol abuse
2) Drug abuse
3) Loss of interest in everyday tasks
4) Eating too much (putting on weight)
5) During the autumn and winter seasons you can be more prone to colds, flu and infections
6) Experience severe periods of sadness
7) Lack of sleep
8) Changes in mood
9) Anxiety (panic attacks)

10) Lack of concentration

11) Lack of socializing (not wanting to mix with people)

Someone who is S.A.D doesn't consider other peoples' feelings. Ever since the 1980s' doctors and scientists have been trying to research S.A.D, the effects and what causes it.

Serotonin is a compound that occurs throughout the body tissue, especially the brain, intestinal tissue and blood platelets. The Serotonin compound acts as a Neurotransmitter and a powerful Vasoconstrictor

Melatonin is a hormone which when released causes the Pineal gland to cause us to sleep. When it is light this Melatonin gland stops producing and this is when we wake up. This procedure also occurs in animals too. Melatonin is a hormone secreted by the Pineal gland during the hours of darkness that induces sleepiness and is thought to have useful applications, e.g. in the treatment of jet lag.

People that suffer from S.A.D especially in the winter feel like hibernating like a hedgehog or tortoise. Someone that suffers from Seasonal Affective Disorder can suffer from a disrupted body clock. I have good nights and bad nights for sleeping.

No one really knows why some people suffer from S.A.D. Some possible triggers of S.A.D can be from the birth of a child (Postnatal Depression), hormonal disruptions to life and Hysterectomy. S.A.D can develop at any age but usually between the ages of 18 and 30., not usually later in life, however, sometimes this can be later in life. Usually, this occurs more in women than men. However, some men don't always let their feelings show or admit to depressive feelings.

There are treatments available for people who suffer from S.A.D. Before you decide what's best for you consult your doctor for advice. There is a treatment called "Bright light therapy". There are different types of light you can use such as:

1) A light visor, which is portable and fits on the head.

2) Light boxes, which range in size either like a TV, tabletop box, or a wall-mounted window type feature which contains tubes and a cover over it.

3) A dawn simulator which is connected to your alarm clock by your bedside allowing a sunrise effect to occur which will wake you up naturally.

There are certain things you can do to improve your condition they are:

1) Expose yourself to more natural light, go out and about more
2) Eat well and do regular exercise
3) Avoid stress. However, this is easier said than done. Try and avoid unnecessary stress during the winter months. You can do this by trying to live a simple life without too many pressures.
4) Take time out to pamper yourself and maybe treat yourself to a professional massage. Try to do relaxation exercises. We have learnt what S.A.D is and how to cope with it.

In chapter 3 of this book, we will discuss how family and friends can understand depression.

CHAPTER 3

HOW CAN FAMILY AND FRIENDS UNDERSTAND DEPRESSION?

When a family member or friend finds out that someone close to them has this illness they tend to shy away from patients, I can't understand why. It's not an illness you can catch. You can never see if a person has it because it is a mental illness, not a physical one.

Sometimes when a family member is ill other members of the household can worry or get distressed because they don't understand what's happening. It may be helpful if family members or friends do research on the subject, to get to know more about the illness, so they will be able to sympathize with the one that is ill. Some children have parents that are Bipolar and they don't understand what is wrong with mom or dad.

My ex-husband brought my little girl into the hospital for visits so I could keep in contact with her. I vaguely remember she was quite young about 2 or 3. She is now 13 and has a better understanding of my illness whereas before she used to shy away from me. Now me and Lydia have bonded just like super glue.

When friends and family care for family or relatives it can become very distressing to their lives. Sometimes someone who is suffering from depression can often shy away from their feelings and simply withdraw from family and friends. Try to get your family member or friend to open up about their feelings and get treatment. You should never blame them for their condition, it's an illness, after all, everyone gets sick. You can help by being positive.

When someone you know is depressed and they need a carer, you can show that you care by being a good listener. Listen to their needs, be sympathetic or spend time with them.

Before someone can take care of a person with depression, they must first take care of themselves. It can be rather frustrating at times when someone you care for is sick, however, by supporting your friend or relative, it can build blocks and make the relationship stronger like cement.

The last thing a person with depression needs is for someone to say "snap out of it". It can be very hurtful. If someone says "pull yourself together", that is just as bad. One of the worst sayings is "cheer up it will never happen".

When speaking with someone who is depressed don't just talk about their illness that can be depressing and make matters worse. Talk about other things you used to enjoy before you got sick. When you are experiencing depression, treat yourself with kindness. The same applies to someone who lives with someone who is depressed. Try to pursue activities together as a family. I try and keep as active as I possibly can. Try to be more sociable, try and do things that you enjoy in your leisure time. Swimming or walking can be very good for you and they help you relax and unwind.

It isn't anybody's fault that you are ill, nor is it your fault you are up or down in the dumps. Life just doesn't cease simply because someone is depressed. If you eat well and take in regular exercise this may help you on the road to recovery.

A carer needs to be able to look after themselves before they can look after someone who is depressed. Carers need to take time out for themselves as well as looking after someone they care about. If someone wants to help you, let them.

Try and take time out doing something pleasurable such as reading, singing or listening to music or whatever it is that you enjoy. People with manic depression also deserve to be happy as well as folk that are already experiencing happiness.

Usually, when someone suffers from depression they tend to disappear from the family and social scene. When people shy away from your illness it doesn't mean that they don't care, it's very often the case that they don't know what to do.

Many people feel like not eating when they are depressed, they seem to lose their appetite. You may find that some of your family members or friends cannot share your pain; however, this doesn't mean they don't care about you. When other people in the family or a friend shies away from a relationship breakdown or bereavement because they are uncomfortable with the grief, this doesn't mean that their feelings are wrong, however, it can be very hurtful to the other party.

What you eat or drink affects your mood. What we eat affects our moods and energy levels which affect fluctuations in your blood sugar levels. Our brains produce chemicals which affect the way we behave and think this affects what we eat. If we eat a healthy balanced diet we feel good whereas if we eat junk food we feel rotten inside. What we eat can affect your functioning mentally as well as physically.

Caffeine which can be found in coffee, tea, Coca Cola and especially chocolate, are the most modifying drug-related substances in the world. Sometimes we have a cup of tea because it is refreshing or sometimes we have a cup of coffee because we are tired, it can be very stimulating. If you have an odd cup of tea or coffee that isn't bad in itself because it can have positive psychological associations, for example meeting a friend for coffee can have a positive effect on you, it's good to get out and about. However drinking too much caffeine can be bad for you, it can cause depression, nervousness and anxiety, so drink in moderation.

In order to keep fit and healthy, you need to eat regularly because if your blood sugar levels fall and you don't eat you can become ill. I have experienced this because I'm also diabetic so I need to eat regularly otherwise I could end up being sick, like when I had a kidney injury, this was when I was diagnosed with diabetes.

When someone is depressed they may comfort eat by eating foods which they know are bad for them such as chips, burgers, cakes, pies or biscuits etc. It's difficult to change your eating habits especially if you are trying to eat healthier and exercise. If you are obese or overweight it can put your health at risk, so like me, I'm going to be more careful what my body intakes every day. Comfort eating is when you keep dipping into the biscuit tin to make yourself feel better, however, if you feel like this try eating fruit instead, you will soon see that weight come off if you eat healthier meals instead of snacking all the time. Another thing you can do is keep your hands busy and then you won't eat too much of the wrong things. When you become dependent on food it's not a sign you are weak, it's what you put in your stomach that counts. You shouldn't use food to control depression.

What can you do to help yourself?

I have this problem of obesity and I'm not happy about my weight so I have decided to do something about it. I see a doctor, C.P.N and psychiatrist. I need to see what went wrong with my overeating and change my eating habits coupled with plenty of exercise. Changing eating habits doesn't happen overnight, it takes time and effort. Food can be better than a comfort; it can be pleasurable and satisfying. Too much of anything can be bad for you, especially too much alcohol.

You have to remember that alcohol is a depressant, it can give short term relief from depression but this feeling doesn't last forever.

Some people who are depressed feel lonely because they haven't any friends or family to turn to. The word loneliness means unaccompanied, isolated, uninhabited, unfrequented and uncomfortably conscious of being alone.

Loneliness can affect anyone especially those people that are suffering with depression. It's a result of extreme sadness. When depression strikes friends and family sometimes cut themselves off from the one that is suffering from Bipolar Disorder or those that suffer sometimes cut themselves off from family and friends.

How can you stop feeling lonely?

1) You need to get out and about more, meet new friends
2) We need to think differently so we can meet more people socially.

Lonely people often feel negative about themselves.

What can I do to help myself?

1) Join a gym, get fit and healthy, and then you will start to feel better, the new you.
2) You need to spend time discussing with someone about the negative feelings you have and try to change the negatives to positives.
3) Join a mental health group
4) Try going out and meet someone for a drink, this gets you out of the house
5) Make a list of things that you enjoy and do them, especially the things you enjoy doing on your own. Part of the battle against loneliness is about feeling good about being alone sometimes.
6) Go and talk to either a neighbour or someone you know, if you feel you can't accomplish this try telephoning someone for a chat or write a letter to someone you know. If after making all the effort, your efforts are made in vain it's not you that has the problem it's the other person that has the problem.

The climb out of depression isn't an easy one but can be achieved. You need to think positive and like me, you can achieve anything. I don't get depressed very often now only now and again. I feel like a mountain has been lifted from my shoulders. When you are at the top of a mountain it's easy to look down and lose your balance in life but hold onto the rope and you won't fall off the mountain. So if you have family and friends don't let them run away from you let them help you. In order to be successful and happy let people help you.

We have just learnt about how friends and family can help in understanding depression. In the next chapter, we will discuss what the signs and symptoms of depression are.

CHAPTER 4

WHATARE THE SIGNSAND SYMPTOMS OF DEPRESSION?

When depression strikes there are many signs and symptoms to look out for such as:

1) A lack of performance at work
2) You lose interest in things you used to do
3) Self-harming
4) Mood swings that are severely out of character
5) Overeating junk food and not eating healthy foods
6) Lack of sleep
7) Loss of sexual drive
8) Feeling whacked and have no energy
9) Going out more, feeling more creative
10) Seeing and hearing things that other people don't see or hear

I found that I had poor hygiene and I didn't feed on the right foods. For someone that suffers from all ten or one symptom of depression, they need help. A depressed person can have feelings of worthlessness, guilt, blaming self for illness and having episodes of self harming.

I remember I did this in hospital on one occasion. I went totally crazy and smashed some plates onto the floor, ran into the garden and cut myself several times thinking that this would solve all my problems but it didn't. I sometimes had morbid thoughts of suicide and tried once to take my own life, l felt I'd let Lydia down as a mum, me being the way I was feeling.

I also remember I suffered from hallucinations at home and this scared the living daylights out of me. Sometimes someone who is manic has very little sleep, perhaps only 3 or 4 hours a night at the most or sometimes you can go nights without sleep. I must admit now I'm a lot stabler within myself, I can sleep better.

Some people are Hypo manic which simply means that a person is in a mild or moderate state. Many people who are in a Hypomanic state can feel good about themselves. Hypomanics can also experience episodes of violence. If this mental state isn't treated soon then the person that has Hypomania can be ill for a few days or for years at a time.

When someone appears in this state they can become quite tearful and may experience racing thoughts and a depressive mood. Some people feeling like this can feel like a failure in life and also have grandiose ideas.

Mixed states of mania is where symptoms of a manic episode coincide with clinical depression in a simultaneous way. It can become quite dangerous when panic disorders, suicide attempts and other complications take root.

I have memory lapses due to having E.C.T (electroconvulsive therapy) several years ago. I am happy to think that these days that this sort of treatment doesn't occur very often now.

Some people who suffer from Bipolar are very creative in a various number of ways. In my case, I feel I can do almost anything I set my mind out to do. I am very creative in writing poetry, knitting and making jewellery. I also enter lots of crossword competitions.

The cause of Bipolar can vary from different people. Some people have family members that suffer from Bipolar, it can also be a genetic thing in the family. In my case, it wasn't genetic.

According to my research, 1969 is when mania first became known. The studies became inconsistent. For some people Bipolar is heredity. There have been many findings that some adults have experienced or have found to be traumatic during childhood such as abusive experiences. Childhood experiences of mania and stressfulness are higher in children than adults. We have analysed the signs and symptoms of depression, we are now going to find out what causes Bipolar Disorder.

CHAPTER 5

WHAT CAUSES BIPOLAR DISORDER?

Very little is known about the causes of depression, some people know why they are depressed some don't know. Both men and women experience mood swings that affect the body's chemistry. Sometimes women that have had babies experience hormonal problems after the birth of a child. It's supposed to be one of the happiest days of a mothers' life. The birth of a child however for some women clutching their newborn child brings nothing but sheer sadness.

Depression, like many other illnesses, can cause you to have the stuffing knocked out of you so you can't cope. What we eat and drink can have an effect on our bodies, in a good way or bad way. We need microbes in our body in order to stay healthy and fit. There are chemicals in our food, water and in the air we breathe. We need to be careful that we don't reach a burnout stage where our body tells us that it's so stressed out that it can't cope when put under pressure. This can happen to anyone.

Some things that can cause depression and stress are:

1) A divorce
2) Moving house
3) Problems at work
4) Problems with kids

If we are going to succeed in combating depression, we need to recognise stress levels

If we are going to succeed in combating depression, we need to recognise stress levels and make a strategic plan to succeed. It's mostly women more than men that get depressed because of hormonal imbalances. Depression is a complicated illness to understand.

Although it has been said that Bipolar is a genetic illness and runs in the family. Some people don't have a history of Bipolar, you may be the only one in your household that is suffering.

Women who are especially pregnant need to be aware that the developing foetus needs the mothers' nutrition in order to keep physically and mentally fit and survive the birth.

If you lead a stressful life, then Bipolar Disorder can be linked to various symptoms like:

1) Childbirth
2) Money problems
3) Relationship problems

You need to try and lead a stress-free life, try to live a simple life with no complications. This in itself isn't easy but can be achieved.

Some people believe that Bipolar is a result of an emotional damage caused earlier in life such as:

1) Emotional abuse
2) Physical abuse
3) Sexual abuse

It's also a shock to the system when you lose someone you love; trauma, grief and neglect can contribute to high unbearable stress levels. You need to try and unwind like a yoyo Sometimes Bipolar affects people with overwhelming problems in daily life. Some people with mania experience a sense of self-importance in the world

Sometimes mental health problems can occur genetically in families. There could be events in your life that have caused the breakdown in your health. It all points to stress and the way we deal with it. If someone is depressed sometimes they are affected by lack of sleep, feel anxious or change their eating habits by eating junk food.

Our moods determine whether we are up or down and are linked to changes that are made in the brains' chemistry, sometimes these changes are astronomical to the person affected.

Symptoms of depression can be controlled by medication such as Lithium. I was on this tablet for quite a while; however, I had to come off it because it started to poison my blood, I wasn't taking in enough fluids. This tablet doesn't suit everyone. If you take this tablet make sure you drink plenty of water otherwise it won't do its job properly.

Stress in life is the most significant factor to mental illness. There are many side effects from taking Lithium they are:

1) Feeling uncontrollably thirsty
2) Passinzg more urine than usual
3) 3) Weight gain
4) Blurred vision
5) Muscles going weak
6) Diarrhoea
7) Twitching muscles
8) Trembling hands
9) Feeling confused
10) Feeling poorly, being sick

Not everyone experiences side effects, many people are alright. If you are not careful you can have too much Lithium in the blood. If you experience any of these symptoms consult your doctor IMMEDIATELY, you will more than likely have to have blood tests to ascertain the problem. Although the causes of Bipolar are not widely known, it varies from individual to individual. It has been said that Bipolar is an abnormality in the brains' functioning.

What can you do to help yourself?

1) Eat a balanced thought out diet
2) Talk to a friend or family member or a medical person
3) Plenty of physical exercise
4) Writing about your experiences
5) Regular relaxation exercises
6) Medication
7) Meditation
8) Make changes in your lifestyle
9) The need to feel wanted and valued

We have just learnt what some of the causes of depression are and what to do to help yourself. Now we are going to discuss Phobias relating to Panic attacks. What are they and how can you cope?

CHAPTER 6

PHOBIAS RELATING TO PANIC ATTACKS

WHAT ARE THEY AND HOW CAN YOU COPE?

What is a phobia?

The word phobia means an irrational fear of something unnecessary. The body and mind can't differentiate between fear and anxiety. The body reacts the same way. This causes the flight or fight syndrome. The body reacts to fear, the hormone adrenaline pumps blood around the body so you breathe faster and have shortness of breath. A phobia is when what you're frightened of causes muscles to tighten up. It closes down the digestive system making you sick, it reduces blood to the eyes causing distorted vision and affects hearing which causes lightheadedness. A phobia is like having a panic attack. The panic attacks can cause you to have spasms so they reach different parts of the body such as:

1) The breast-bone
2) The spine
3) The face
4) The arms
5) The groins
6) The toes and the rest of the body

The symptoms related to panic attacks are:

1) Shortness of breath
2) Feeling terrified
3) Feeling weak
4) Feeling the urge to go to the toilet
5) To lose control of self

6) Having sweaty palms

7) Feeling dizzy

8) Feeling nausea

9) Trembling

10) Having palpitations

Phobias can affect anyone regardless of social standing, intelligence, education or wealth (With the exception of animal phobias) and tend to occur in young adulthood. They affect women more than men and are more common among sensitive or intelligent people.

Common animal phobias such as:

1) Spiders

2) Mice

3) Snakes

4) Rats

5) Dogs

There are other common phobias such as:

1) Agoraphobia (fear of open or public spaces)

2) Claustrophobia (which is fear of being in closed or confined spaces)

3) Social phobias (Fears to do with social contact)

I personally suffer from Agoraphobia, lightning, thunder, fear of the dark, fear of spiders and the wind. I walk backwards in a headwind. Sometimes phobias start because of depression, moving house or a traumatic event that occurred during childhood.

Some people that suffer from depression, especially severe clinical depression, can suffer from phobias too. When I'm in a small confined space like a lift or small room it can cause me to experience a panic attack resulting in my heart accelerating like a car. I can sometimes become lightheaded, disoriented and dizzy.

Someone who suffers from a panic attack can feel anxious and afraid so adrenalin pumps into the bloodstream making the heart accelerate faster. Sometimes when you experience a panic attack you can hyperventilate.

According to Mind "One in three suffers from panic attacks". Someone who suffers from panic attacks can find them very frightening. Some people can suffer from five or up to twenty minutes from an attack.

Someone who suffers from Bipolar (manic depression) can also suffer from panic attacks, diabetes, asthma, or anxiety attacks. When you have a panic attack it can cause the following symptoms such as:

1) Breathlessness
2) A racing heart
3) Pains in the chest
4) Fainting/ dizziness
5) Numbness in the joints
6) Hot and cold flushes
7) Feeling sick
8) Fear of choking
9) Fear that the world will end
10) Fear of dying
11) Feeling isolated/ cut off from the world
12) Feeling crazy

Some physical causes of panic attacks:

1) Blood sugars unsteady as a result of a poor diet or from fasting
2) Hyperventilation which means over-breathing, stress, and not enough oxygen reaching the body
3) Problems digesting food
4) Some anti-depressants are not used because they can cause panic attacks
5) Alcohol, cigarettes, caffeine and drugs can cause panic attacks
6) Sometimes Drug withdrawal symptoms can cause increased anxiety and stress
7) Sometimes the brain doesn't function properly, it's called Organ Brains Dysfunction. This affects balance coordination and can affect visual difficulties which can cause stress and Agoraphobia
8) Panic attacks can cause pain and discomfort

What to do if you have a panic attack:

Breathe into a paper bag slowly, not quickly, because it can cause you to breathe out too much Carbon dioxide.

HOW TO PREVENTAPANICATTACK

1) Try not to get stressed
2) Changing your way of life such as: healthy eating, regular exercise, better sleep patterns, relaxation and keeping occupied, especially using your hands; for e.g. gardening or knitting. If you are Diabetic remember to do your sugar readings.
3) Don't keep your worries to yourself. Speak to someone in confidence i.e. G.P, family member or close friend.
4) Try to cope the best way you can by taking an anxiety management course. In my first book Snappy but Happy – Revised edition you will find helpful steps to recover.
5) Join a support group. I joined a Mind group at least once a week and also I've joined a knitting group at 99.2 Hermitage FM.
6) Breathe from the diaphragm, not the chest.
7) Do relaxation classes or put on a tape to unwind.
8) Look at the positive things in your life.
9) When you have a panic attack, tell yourself that you are not dying and do what I do, pray for help to cope with the attacks
10) If you have a panic attack, try and keep calm and relax your breathing then you will feel less tense.

Here are some useful organizations:

www.anxietyuk.org.uk www.firststeps.org www.nopanic.org.uk

PANIC ATTACKS: HOW TO HELP YOURSELF

1) Take control of your symptoms, you have the power to do this.
2) You need to accept that the panic attack is a part of your illness and a part of you. Try to reassure yourself everything will be ok, you will not die and it's not the end of the world. Panic attacks can be embarrassing too.
3) People that suffer from panic attacks often have a vivid imagination. You can train your mind to focus on the sense of well-being. I go to a relaxation expert and she helps me to relax.

4) Learn to do relaxation techniques. They can be from books, c.ds or a therapist

5) Avoid hyperventilation as this can cause a panic attack

6) Eat healthy foods and at least three good meals a day. Avoid sugary drinks/foods especially if you are Diabetic unless your blood sugar goes right down below 4

7) Eat potatoes, rice, pasta and plenty of fruit and vegetables

8) When panic attacks occur hold a paper bag over the nose and mouth, breathing into the bag and out again, it helps relieves symptoms

We have discussed Phobias relating to panic attacks and how to cope. We are now going to discuss: How can you cope with being admitted to hospital?

CHAPTER 7

HOW CAN YOU COPE WITH BEING ADMITTED TO HOSPITAL?

When someone is suffering from severe mental health problems they can admit themselves voluntarily to hospital. In real severe cases when someone is assessed to be at risk to themselves or others they can be detained under the mental health act.

Sometimes people who have the tendency to harm themselves or others are sectioned before they are admitted to hospital for their own protection and that of others.

In a hospital environment, there are set times for meals. Patients can help themselves to drinks at any time during the day. Medication can often cause the mouth to become dry, so regular fluids are needed in order to prevent dehydration. Medication is usually prescribed after a meal and before bedtime. First admission to hospital can be very frightening to begin with. I've been through this ordeal. I remember when I was admitted to hospital it was very daunting and scary at first, being surrounded by poorly people.

When people that suffer from Bipolar are high they feel on top of the world. The hospital environment tries to make people feel comfortable and at ease - although some people, like me, find hospitals scary. Upon first entering the hospital a patient can, by request, ask for a locker to put valuables in safekeeping.

During many of my hospital stays there were things to do to keep you occupied such as pottery and gardening. I planted some Japanese onions. I also made my own breakfast and did relaxation classes. I also went to music karaoke classes on a Friday.

Sometimes when I was in hospital I listened to music or did some knitting, which I also enjoy, it is so relaxing and has a calming effect upon me. When I was in hospital I coped the best way I could, I met some really nice people. When I was first admitted to hospital I was very apprehensive to start with, however, I soon got the help I needed, in the nick of time. I was relieved to be honest when I was admitted because at least family and friends wouldn't worry about me.

In hospital a person who suffers from a mental illness such as: Bipolar Disorder (manic depression) and can't cope can be admitted voluntarily, however, if you voluntarily submit yourself to hospital you can go home at any time except when you need to be detained for health reasons, then you can be detained for 72 hours until seen by a doctor/ psychiatrist or nurse. The outcome will depend on the medical expert whether you can go home or not.

If someone's condition is serious under the mental health act they can be sectioned which means they cannot discharge themselves from hospital. When someone is sectioned at least three people i.e. two doctors and a mental health practitioner have to decide whether to pursue this cause of action or not.

When someone is sectioned in hospital it can feel like a person's whole life is taken from them, your power of reasoning is overruled and you can't think about making decisions anymore. It's like a thick fog with no end in sight. When I was sectioned for six months it felt like I was serving a prison sentence, which had been imposed on me by the powers that be.

Some family members feel guilty because their loved one had to be sectioned, however, it is also a sigh of relief to them also because they know that they are being cared for and are in the best place.

In a psychiatric hospital people that suffer from Bipolar Disorder (manic depression) or any other illness, have their own named nurse that takes care of them. They also have a Consultant psychiatrist that takes care of them whether they are in hospital or out of hospital.

Each psychiatric ward in the hospital has a ward manager, and a deputy manager who takes charge when the manager is off work.

After a patient has been sectioned for a while, he or she may be allowed home for a day's leave, if this is successful more days' at home would then be allowed, until finally the section can be lifted and eventually a person can be discharged from hospital. When I was in hospital my finances were in a mess, I needed a social worker to help me sort things out.

Hospitals have their pros and cons. Sometimes people are terrified at the thought of being admitted to hospital, this is usually the last resort. Doctors/psychiatrists (nurses) try to keep their patients out of hospital by providing alternative care i.e. medication review. Sometimes a crisis intervention/ crisis resolution or crisis team is put in place.

When I was first admitted to hospital it was very daunting and I started to feel the strain, I had feelings of despair because I was away from home, however I soon settled down to the hospital routine, it had become my second home, because I had been in hospital for quite some time I got to know the nursing staff of Ashby ward in Glenfield Leicester, they were all so nice to me and I'll never forget that. The hospital had become a place of safety and healing to me, a start on a road to stability. When being admitted to hospital, it can give you space to breathe and chill out. A hospital can be a safe haven, also to people that
self-harm; it can become a place of healing to the afflicted, a place of tranquility to those troubled and have a calming effect. There are people in the hospital that have problems like mine, however everyone is in the same boat and needs help, hospital can become a

Place of peace and quiet... When you are in hospital you don't have the pressures of the outside world to deal with.

For people who are severely manic, having Bipolar Disorder, and are hospitalized, they need to find out more about their condition. You can understand more about your condition by recognizing the early warning signs and developing ways of coping with them. I find music very soothing for the soul. When you are in hospital, it's a chance for your medication to be reviewed and stabilized. Family, friends and medical professionals can submit their input towards your treatment and hopefully help you on the road to recovery.

CHAPTER 8

HOW CAN YOU COPE WITH SLEEP PROBLEMS AND DEPRESSION?

The average person needs seven or eight hours of sleep at night in order to feel refreshed and renewed for the next day, however, some people need more sleep, about ten hours or more whereas some people do less than five hours a day.

In fact, the amount of sleep we need changes by our age whereas small babies on average spend most of their time sleeping, this promotes growth... Children need at least nine or ten hours a day.

When we sleep it's like a cycle of light or deep sleep. At the end of each cycle of sleep, we start to experience a different kind of sleep which is called R.E.M (rapid eye movement) when we dream. This experience isn't harmful to a person, in fact, it's totally the opposite, and it's important for your well-being and gives restoration to the brain. During sleep, a growth hormone is released and this is how growth starts, hence whereas old people need less sleep than younger people.

Some people may lose a good nights' sleep, this in itself isn't harmful, in fact, some people can go for days without sleep, and this too is perfectly ok because most people can return to a normal sleeping pattern. However, for some people, they can feel fatigued and irritable because they can't get back to a normal sleep pattern. Some people find it difficult in concentrating at times and it can become dangerous to people who drive or operate machinery.

In fact, sleep deprivation or (insomnia) can cause psychological changes in our behaviour. Lack of sleep for many days at a time can cause someone to make mistakes or act irrationally. It is called sleep debt.

Sometimes people that go to bed end up worried about something, can't relax, so you end up tossing and turning throughout the night which ends up in you getting only two or three hours sleep. This irritability or depression can affect everything and everyone in your life. Insomnia means sleeplessness or a prolonged ability to sleep. Insomnia can also refer to a sleepless night or waking up in the night and not being able to get back to sleep.

There are millions of people who suffer from sleep problems; they need to consult a doctor to get help, with the need of tranquillizers or sleeping tablets. This is also part of my illness, sleep deprivation (insomnia). I can go without several nights of sleep for days at a time but feel really agitated, irritable and have a lack of energy. Poor sleep can affect anyone at any age. Poor sleep can be hazardous to your health.

In fact, there are millions of people, adults and especially teenagers that suffer from sleep disorders. When someone suffers from Insomnia they can't function properly. Sleep is important to your well-being. Getting a good nights' sleep adds to a good quality of life.

In fact, famous pianist George Shearing who was blind from birth and many other famous people were studied because they seemed to display the same brain-wave patterns during the dreaming period, however, George Shearing dreamed of sounds instead of sights, this was during R.E.M (rapid eye movement).

It's interesting to note that doctors from sleep clinics say that Insomnia isn't a disease, it's a symptom. It's also a known fact that there are different types of Insomnia and different types of causes. You need to find out which Insomnia you have, some people say take a pill and you'll be ok, however, that's not always the solution. I've been on sleeping tablets for at least eleven years, sometimes they work, sometimes they don't. It's trial and error.

I've tried drinking milky drinks before bed, however, this doesn't always work. In this chapter, we are going to see how we can cope with sleep problems so that you can eventually have no more sleepless nights.

Each person with Insomnia suffers differently from the next person. It's good to analyse your own sleep behavioural patterns and see whether there is a direct pattern to your failure of sleep. Some of the things you can do to help yourself are:

1) Look at your diet; see if you can improve in your eating habits
2) Exercise regularly
3) Watch your stress levels
4) Do relaxation exercises
5) Keep a diary of your sleep patterns i.e. how long you sleep and what goes on through the night

If you follow the guidelines in this book you will start to feel better, learn to relax and have a good nights' sleep, which is a part of everyday life, and is essential to your physical/ mental well-being.

Famous painters and sculptures such as Picasso and Michael Angelo have made it a part of art. Usually, eight hours of sleep is enough to rejuvenate the body and mind for the next day.

When animals are asleep in R.E.M (dream sleep) they often act out their dreams, they may hiss, crouch, scratch and fight whilst asleep. In humans, a similar thing happens, although we don't hiss, crouch, or scratch we may act out our dreams by becoming violent during this period of sleep without realizing it.

When we sleep a lot, things go on without us realizing it, for one thing, during the first couple of hours or so the heart /blood pressure goes down. When we are in R.E.M the blood pressure goes down slightly as this is a rest period in your life. When we sleep our blood is directed to our muscles in the body. During R.E.M sleep when we are dreaming, the brain becomes alive pumping more blood into the body.

Sleep debt can cause the brain to slow down; it can cause irritability, lack of concentration, erratic behaviour and memory loss.

In fact, a sleep researcher is quoted as saying Insomnia is much more than losing a few nights' sleep". There are some famous people who have been known to suffer from Insomnia such as Marilyn Monroe, Cary Grant, Charles Dickens, author Jacqueline Susan, Benjamin Franklin, Napoleon Bonaparte and Winston Churchill, just to name a few.

There are different types of Insomnia such as:

1) People that don't go to bed at bedtime
2) People that go to sleep but can't stay asleep

It's a good idea to keep a sleep diary just like you would a food diary. You need to analyse your sleep patterns. One way you can keep a check of your sleep is by keeping track of the time you go to bed and the time you get up. You may also need to know how long it roughly takes you to fall asleep. Once you've figured it out, you need to distinguish how often you wake up from sleep.

I often find that once I've found I'm awake, I can't get back to sleep again. In fact, I've been sleeping with the aid of sleeping tablets for several years now. You need to keep a track of your sleep patterns each night. Lack of sleep usually makes me feel exhausted for the rest of the day. Accidents have been known to happen because of lack of sleep, this can happen at home or in the workplace. I have been known to catnap during the day; sometimes I stay in bed for longer periods. I believe my Insomnia started after the birth of Lydia, my daughter, since then I haven't been able to sleep properly without the aid of sleeping tablets. I've had to rely on tablets to get me to sleep at night. Sometimes when I'm in bed I toss and turn all night, ending up with the bedclothes on the floor in the morning. My husband says that I'm a heavy breather during sleep. Let your body determine how much sleep you need.

Let someone who suffers from Insomnia and depression get the professional help they need. Usually, the treatment for depression and Insomnia can very often solve an Insomniac problem. Sometimes it's good to analyse yourself by asking questions such as:

1) Have you been feeling sad for quite some time?
2) Do you feel that the future is hopeless?
3) Do you find yourself crying uncontrollably?
4) Have you stopped looking after your appearance?

If you answer yes to these questions you may have a sleep problem with depression.

Poor sleep can cause your mood to fluctuate from one minute you're up, the next minute you're down. In fact, medical illnesses such as back pain, coughs, and headaches are just a few mentioned which can cause a poor lack of sleep. Insomnia can be an added problem and sometimes lead to Kidney/ Thyroid disease, so keep an eye on your sleep patterns. In order to function properly, we all need to work, rest and play, just like a Mars bar.

Regular exercise promotes sleep. There are certain things that you can do to eliminate sleep disorders such as:

1) Reduce caffeine intake
2) Avoid smoking
3) Limit alcohol intake

According to a famous sleep specialist at the sleep disorder clinic in 1995, he indicated that patients with Insomnia have a 9% metabolic rate during day and night as supposed to people who don't have Insomnia. Daily drinking more than three cups of coffee a day can cause the Insomniac to make their condition worse.

Many people use alcohol as an aid to Insomnia; however, this doesn't get rid of the problem. There are certain dangers of using alcohol to make you sleep. Alcohol promotes a poor sleep pattern and also you can become totally dependent on it. You should never forget this motto:

Alcohol and sleeping tablets don't mix.

Smoking can also cause Insomnia; it's the nicotine that keeps you awake. Smoking can cause the blood pressure to rise. Sometimes people who smoke experience withdrawal symptoms during the night. People that are trying to give up smoking need to stay away from people who smoke and buy healthy snacks to avoid the craving of smoke.

These suggestions are to help you with your Insomnia:

1) You need to cut your sleep time down. After you have achieved this you will start to feel the benefits.
2) Never try to force the issue of sleep; if you need sleep, it should happen even if you take sleeping tablets. You need to feel comfortable in bed; you will find you rest more easily. I sometimes listen to music, this helps me to relax and unwind. Reading in bed can sometimes make you feel sleepy. The worst thing an Insomniac can do is worry about it.

Many Insomniacs have a low self-esteem of themselves. In fact, some celebrities such as Mark Twain dealt with it with humour, he said "If you can't sleep, try lying on the edge of the bed, then you might drop off."

Lewis Carroll, author of Alice in Wonderland was also a mathematical genius. To help him sleep, he used to do mathematical puzzles to ease his mind.
Roman poet Horace coined the phrase "I cannot sleep a wink".

3) Some people have things that they do to make themselves relax and comfortable. The Insomniac can become addicted to the sleeping pill. I'm still taking it, after 11yrs of my illness.

It is a well-known fact, that Charles Dickens was known to move his bed, wherever he slept so that his head pointed north and his feet pointed south; he believed that currents would flow through his body, a strange notion.

4) You need to give yourself enough time to unwind from the days/ experiences. Do something like a hobby to make you relax.

A certain celebrity such as Burt Reynolds said " I am a great believer in a hot bath and hot tubs are the most underrated things in the world."

A famous doctor of the institute of California Santa Barbara backs up this statement made by Burt Reynolds stating that people who have been into a hot tub before bedtime have fallen asleep faster than people who don't have a hot tub. Another way to wind down is to have a massage by someone close to you. It can be very therapeutic.

Try to live a fruitful life, nothing too stressful. If you keep yourself physically and mentally active you will feel tired and want to sleep.

5) Try having a short nap during the day. Many people feel that they can't sleep at night so they cat nap, this isn't harmful in itself, however, it helps aid a good nights' sleep and you feel more relaxed.

The following are aids to help an Insomniac:

1) Only use your bed for sleeping
2) Go to bed when you are almost asleep, not just when you are feeling tired
3) Stay up until you are sleepy, then go back to bed
4) You need to set your alarm to the same time every day, to get your body/ mind active for the days' activities
5) Don't cat nap unless you have too
6) Never try to force yourself to sleep
7) Do relaxation techniques i.e. listen to a recording of a relaxation tape to help you unwind
8) You need to keep your sleep schedule in order to see your progress

Before going to bed you need to learn to do relaxation techniques. Some Insomniacs do actually benefit from using relaxation tapes to help them unwind. Doing gentle exercises before sleep can really benefit you, and help you to relax.

Meditation is a state of quietness which decreases the activity of the nervous system, it helps to reduce tension. You can reduce the stress in your life by changing the way you look at things.

Sleep patterns can be affected by what you eat. The University of Chicago compared the effects of sleep on certain snacks during the night several people found that a milky drink of Ovaltine was very beneficial at bedtime and made them feel sleepy.

Cats have also been known to sleep better after they have had milk in their stomachs. Changing your eating habits to healthier foods can reduce sleep debt. People that are on diets which lack proper nutrients, also find that they are sometimes suffering from fatigue, Insomnia, Irritability and Depression.

For a healthy diet try the following:

1) Eat salad & fresh fruit
2) Eat whole-grain fibre foods such as wholemeal bread and unsweetened cereals and vitamin B
3) Reduce your fat intake
4) Eat less meat but more fish
5) Bake, boil, roast or steam food
6) Eat 2 or 3 eggs per week
7) Limit your alcohol/caffeine intake. Cutting down on alcohol and caffeine can help you sleep better.
8) Eat plenty fresh vegetables

If you eat a heavy meal at night, this can keep you awake at night. In order to ensure a good nights' sleep you need a good breakfast and lunch, also eat a light tea so that you can sleep soundly. Eating poultry or fish with your evening meal can promote a good nights' sleep.

If you feel hungry during the night, rather than cooking an extra meal, provide yourself with a healthy snack. Try taking vitamin B which includes iron, copper, zinc, magnesium and calcium. Vitamin B12 is also a good help. Although vitamin B doesn't suit everyone, some people find that it acts as a stimulation and aids sleeplessness. Amino acids are found in food and are responsible for building blocks which help the body build proteins. This process is called Tryptophan. It can be found in the following foods:

1) Milk
2) Meat
3) Fish
4) Poultry
5) Eggs

6) Bacon

7) Beans

8) Peanuts

This Tryptophan is very important to our sleep, it's the brains' transmitters that slow down the nervous system when approaching sleep. In fact, many people recommend taking herbal remedies for sleep. You can get herbal tea from the supermarket.

Exercise is a very important part of a day, although exercise doesn't guarantee a good nights' sleep, it can help. Any exercise is good for you. Usually, the recommendation for exercise is 4 or 5 hours a week. It's usually after 2 or 3 hours of vigorous exercise that you will start to see any positive results. Regular exercise can promote a good nights' sleep.

If you have Insomnia it's recommended that you still get up at the same time each day, so that your body clock may eventually get back to normal. Sometimes physical pain can keep you awake, like a headache or toothache. People that are Insomniacs and suffer from depression can often wake up early in the morning but have trouble getting back to sleep. Sleeping pills aren't the long term solution to sleep problems. Taking sleeping tablets can be a force of habit to some because people feel that if they didn't take their tablets the sleeplessness would become much worse. It's a vicious circle. Taking sleeping tablets cannot improve your mentality; in fact, they slow you down.

If your Insomnia lasts more than 6 months continue to see your G.P. Sleep problems can affect people at work, so there is danger of accidents happening. Sometimes lack of sleep can cause jeopardy in the workplace or in social relationships. Some people find it difficult to stay awake during the day because of previous lack of sleep during the night. Some people experience forgetfulness or disorientation with sleep problems. If you have any of these problems then you need to consult your G.P Poor sleep can be as a result of a medical problem. If you experience stress or anxiety problems consult a stress management consultant or psychiatrist or G.P.

How can I help myself?

!) If you need to use sleeping tablets use them, only as prescribed by a doctor

9) Learn to relax and the panic of sleep will pass over you

10) If you have an overactive mind, listen to relaxing noises such as music

11) If you have overworked yourself, don't lie in bed worrying about it

12) Panic is inspired by thoughts so don't overload your brain, learn to relax.

13) Noises in your head can't harm you so if you suffer from this ignore them

We have just learnt how to cope with sleep problems and depression, now we will discuss how to cope with suicidal feelings and how to cope with someone who is suicidal.

CHAPTER 9

HOW CAN YOU COPE WITH SUICIDAL FEELINGS? & HOW CAN YOU HELP SOMEONE WHO IS SUICIDAL?

When someone is suicidal they may experience feelings of sheer terror. Someone who is suicidal has feelings of hopelessness and despair. Some people feel that they haven't anything to live for anymore. Some people may experience feelings of guilt or failure in their lives and this triggers feelings of suicide. Sometimes you might feel that you can't talk to anyone about how you feel, you may think that family and friends wouldn't understand you.

Many people who feel suicidal neglect their personal appearance i.e. seldom washing, you can also lose a lot of sleep and find yourself awake all night.

Some people find a deep satisfaction by cutting, burning or biting themselves, believe me this isn't the answer to your problems. Some people that resort to suicide act on impulse and don't think about the consequences of their actions.

Some people have suicidal feelings because they are in debt, they can no longer control what happens in their lives. You may suffer from loneliness, lose your job, or suffer from bereavement.

Very often is the case that people with mental health problems can resort to suicide. Some people have found these organizations useful:

1) Mind
2) Depression Alliance
3) Hearing Voices Network
4) Papyrus

5) Samaritans

6) Sane

CAN YOU GET HELP?

Yes, you can get help from the above organizations. If you are feeling suicidal take the following steps to prevent these feelings:

1) Talk to your G.P about how you feel, sometimes all you need is a listening ear. Sometimes your G.P may prescribe antidepressants for you, other times, depending on how severe your condition is, you may be transferred to a counsellor, psychotherapist or may even admit you to hospital.

2) Most people admit themselves voluntarily to hospital, however in severe cases where people may be at harm to themselves or others, they are detained under the mental health act.

What everyone needs to know is: How can you help yourself?

1) Speak to family/ friends which can make a big difference to you. When family or friends aren't available, there are other people such as a doctor who can help

2) Don't have too much medication in the house, this avoids the temptation to take all the tablets

3) Learn to relax and chill out. Take up a hobby or do something that will calm you down.

4) Do regular exercise, this will aid a good nights' sleep, you will start to feel healthier too

5) Eat healthier foods, cut out the junk food

6) Keep a log/diary of your achievements such as exercise, food and sleep plan.

7) Learn to express yourself in an artistic way

8) Look at other peoples' experiences. How they got better.

THE BIG QUESTION IS: CAN YOU RECOVER?

Getting better can take a considerable amount of time, also some people don't recover completely, however, if you can get the correct help you need suicidal thoughts can be overcome. Some Bipolar patients may have suicidal feelings. The key is to watch for the early warning signs such as:

1) Talking about suicide

2) Loss of bereavement

3) Risky behaviour

4) Feelings of hopelessness/despair
5) Stop taking medication
6) Lack of poor hygiene, not eating properly
7) Withdrawn/feeling isolated
8) Saving medications (planning to take medications)

It is estimated that around 90% of people that suffer from Bipolar have a psychiatric disorder before they try to commit suicide. Usually people with Bipolar Disorder experience feelings of suicide during periods of their lives when they are unstable. Family members/friends shouldn't feel guilty if the person with Bipolar ends their life, you can't be held responsible for someone else's actions.

Many people attempt suicide because of job loss, family bereavement, and alcohol or drug abuse. You may feel trapped, in a situation you may find impossible to resolve. You may find that there is nothing you can do but run or kill yourself. If you feel like this you need help. You should never ignore someone who is suicidal, help by being a good listener, and encourage them to open up about their feelings.

Try to get them to seek help professionally, you can see a G.P psychiatrist or mental health worker who can give you support in times of distress. The Samaritans are a UK charity that can help anyone suffering from suicidal thoughts/feelings. Bipolar Disorder can have a huge impact on any relationship or especially a spouse.

People with Bipolar are sometimes susceptible to suicidal thoughts; these people have a greater chance of dying by suicide, rather than the population in general.

Sometimes people hear voices, telling them to kill themselves. Some people take their own lives because they are suffering from depression and feel like they are in a hopeless state about the future.

Approximately 70% of recorded suicides are people suffering from depression. Some people experiencing problems in relationships have experienced suicidal thoughts. An interesting fact, attempted suicides are more than likely to occur for the unemployed, rather than for those in employment. It's men that are more prone to commit suicide because they bottle up all their feelings whereas women usually talk openly about their feelings.

YOU MAY NOW BE WONDERING:

WHAT CAN I DO TO HELP?

1) You can show you care by being there for them
2) Talk with them sympathetically by having a listening ear
3) Try and help them solve their problems
4) Accept them and their condition
5) Encourage family/friends to open up and talk to their G.P. He or she will be able to get you some professional help.
6) You need support from family/friends or from useful sources such as the Samaritans
7) In, and only in an emergency, if someone is in danger from suicide and has mental health problems and refuses to get help, then under the mental health act, someone can be treated without their consent.

In order to get help, you need to get help for yourself. If you need support it's essential that you find someone to talk to, someone you can confide in, such as a family or friend or professional mental health worker. Writing out a personal list of contact numbers, this usually does the trick, so that you can get the right help at the right time.

We have discussed how you can cope with suicidal feelings and of course how to help someone who is suicidal. We are now going to discuss how you can improve your mental health and rebuild your life after breakdown.

CHAPTER 10

---◆---

HOW CAN YOU IMPROVE YOUR MENTAL HEALTH? & HOW CAN YOU REBUILD YOUR LIFE AFTER BREAKDOWN?

Displaying good mental health means that you take control of yourself. You look after yourself both physically and mentally. When someone is mentally ill they can still cope by showing that they are in control. In order to get well and keep well you first need to accept and have confidence in yourself. Think positive every day and then you won't go wrong.

In order to keep Bipolar under control, you need to keep stress to a minimum because it's often stress that leads to a mood swing. In order to lead a stress-free life you need to do the following:

1) Relaxation exercises or meditation
2) Eat healthier foods
3) Avoid situations and people that cause stress
4) Restrict or stop smoking
5) Don't take drugs such as Heroin etc.
6) Reduce or stop drinking alcohol
7) Take part in activities you enjoy such as: sports, knitting etc.

Regular sleep can help a Bipolar sufferer to feel better within themselves. It has been said that people that suffer from Bipolar Disorder either sleep too much or not at all. There is a huge link between sleep and depression. If you have enough sleep, it usually helps towards the next day, leaving you relaxed and chilled. It tones the body and helps it to rejuvenate.

Before going to bed you should take your medication, at least 30 minutes before sleep, you might find listening to music a tonic.

In order to combat sleep deprivation, you need to go to bed at the same time each night and wake up at the same time each day as this can help with your body clock getting into a routine. You need at least seven or eight hours of sleep at night. If you go to work try to avoid doing shift work as this knocks your body clock out of sync.

Avoid drinking coffee or tea after 4 pm, and switch to decaffeinated instead. Try taking a relaxing bath and listening to relaxing music. Don't watch TV just before going to bed because this stimulates the brain and keeps you awake.

Physical exercise each day can help with Bipolar symptoms. Acupuncture has been known as a therapy to help people that are clinically depressed. Massage can be very stimulating and helps to reduce stress. Reflexology is very beneficial in helping to deal with depression and other illnesses. I personally have had reflexology and found it very stimulating and beneficial to my wellbeing. Our diet can have a huge impact on our lives, our moods and behavioural patterns. This can also affect your mental health.

If you want to make a big difference to your mental health you need to do the following:

1) Drink less alcohol.
2) Eat more fish, fish is good for the bones and for the skin complexion.
3) Drink less coffee/tea and switch to decaffeinated.
4) Eat fresh fruit/veg.
5) Drink plenty of water.
6) Eat low-fat products such as yoghurt, cheese, margarine etc...
7) Eat nuts/seeds.
8) Don't eat ready dinners/processed food make your own.
9) Eat a good breakfast to start the day.
10) Eat less sugar.

Drinking too much alcohol can affect the brain. Alcohol is known to affect Bipolar sufferers with depression. Drinking excess amounts of alcohol can affect people with Bipolar, it can affect the liver functioning properly. Excessive alcohol can cause you to become aggressive, angry and alcohol is a depressant.

Eating plenty of fish is part of eating a well-balanced diet. Some fish are rich in omega 3 and vitamins which are essential to good general health. You should aim to eat 3-4 portions a week, this promotes a healthy body and is good for the brain.

Drinking fewer amounts of coffee and tea can help control mood swings. Drinking too much of these substances can lead to your nervous system becoming overstimulated, which can increase symptoms of insomnia and anxiousness. Coffee contains a substance called theophylline which is a chemical that disturbs the sleeping pattern. Drinking too much tea isn't good either, because it contains Tannin which prevents the body from absorbing nutrients such as vitamin B. There is nothing wrong with having a couple of tea or coffee drinks a day, providing you don't drink them at night because they may induce mania or insomnia.

Fresh fruit and vegetables are very good for the immune system. It is recommended that you eat five portions of fruit and vegetables a day – prunes, raisins, blackberries, strawberries, raspberries, oranges, grapes, cherries, kiwi fruit, grapefruit, apples, bananas etc… Vegetables – spinach, brussels, broccoli, beetroot, peppers, onion, corn on the cob, aubergines, potatoes, carrots etc…

Drinking plenty of water at least 1.5 litres a day can promote good health and prevent dehydration. Try to drink bottled or filtered water instead of tap water because it's better for you.

Eating low-fat products such as one portion of meat, dairy produce, eggs, beans, lentils, tofu, seeds and nuts is good for you. Try to cut down on carbohydrates such as bread, pasta and potatoes.

Snacking on nuts and seeds is very good for the brain. They contain Omega 3 which is a protecting oil for the brain. Nuts such as walnuts, and seeds such as pumpkin, flax seeds, walnut oil, rapeseed oil, soya beans and leafy green vegetables are very good for you. Try to cut down on ready-made meals because too many of them aren't very good for the brain. Eating too much processed foods can interfere with mood disorders and cause hormonal imbalance. If you have a poor diet it can put increased stress on and affect the liver. It can become sluggish and won't be able to detoxify the body properly.

Deep-fried food is very bad or the cholesterol White bread and pastries n cause problems with the blood sugar such as insomnia, sweating fatigue, irritability, dizziness etc…

Always make sure that you have a decent breakfast to start the day. Breakfast is the most important meal of the day, so you should eat it – even if you only eat a little breakfast this is good for you. If you are prone to miss breakfast this can have a negative effect on your mood. A well-balanced breakfast consists of porridge or wholegrain cereals, berries or other fruit, or perhaps beans or eggs on wholemeal toast (not white).

Are herbal remedies good for you?

Herbal teas, especially camomile, are very good for calmness and sleep. Lemongrass tea is excellent for refreshment, and peppermint tea is very good for indigestion. There are other remedies that are good for you such as dandelion, chicory, and barley tea. Fresh fruit

juices are good, the ones without added sugar are very good. Water is the best source of fluids.

How does alcohol affect the brain? It is the brain's worst enemy. If you drink too much alcohol regularly it can interfere with the liver's functioning. For people suffering from Bipolar Disorder drinking lots of alcohol can depress the nervous system causing behavioural problems such as anger or aggressiveness. If you drink alcohol the Bipolar patient can be affected, the medication ceases to work properly, especially when taking antidepressants.

The looming question is how can you rebuild your life and learn to help yourself?

In order to help yourself i.e. to stop a mood swing from occurring can be in itself quite difficult. You first need to recognize the signs so you can avoid hospitalization. Keep a diary of your life, the things that help you and the things that don't. You need to find out all you can about the illness because there are many organizations that can help you in times of distress, such as the Samaritans. Rethink has really helped me gain confidence in myself and my abilities. I also use a social drop-in run by Mind.

One of the main signs of being depressed is stress. You need to try to avoid getting yourself into stressful situations. If I get stressed I put on a c.d. and this suppresses my anxiousness. It changes my mood to a more calmer state in a relaxed atmosphere.

When I was in hospital I joined a relaxation class and we listened to therapeutic relaxing music. I found this very beneficial to my well-being. It definitely worked for me. When you find something which works for you, keep at it constantly to allow yourself to feel better and content.

A mood swing can affect family and friends, you need to explain to them why you feel the way you do, it's not your fault, it's just your illness, you can't help the way you are. Hopefully, they will understand what a depressed person needs – there is someone they can rely on to help and support them.

When it comes to activities you need to have a balance in your life. Some people with Bipolar Disorder can still go to work, so if this describes you try and have plenty of relaxation, as well as fulfilling your workload. Apart from work you need rest and exercise. Exercise at least 3 times a week, for at least 20 minutes per day.

Life isn't all about work, work, work, it's also about work rest and play – like a Mars bar. You need fun and humour in your life. When was the last time you had a really good laugh? It does you the world of good.

Many people think that they don't need to take their medication because they feel well and are better off without it. I had one of my tablets stopped which resulted in me having no sleep for 5 days. I was soon put back on the tablet.

If you do feel that you have improved in your mental illness consult your G.P. before stopping any medication.

When someone is admitted to hospital for Bipolar, they are entitled to have a say in their treatment. If there is a treatment that you don't agree with, you have the right to refuse and choose other options for your needs. If you are really distressed you can admit yourself voluntarily to hospital. This process is called "informal patient".

If you are really ill and refuse to go to hospital, and it is in your best interests to go in you can be admitted compulsorily under the Mental Health Act. A health official, solicitor, or psychiatrist will be on hand to help you. This process is called "under section".

When someone is first admitted to hospital, like I've said before it can be a daunting experience, even scary.

Some long term patients with depression can be given E.C.T. (electroconvulsive therapy). However, this process isn't done very often now. It can cause short term memory loss, or like in my particular case long term memory loss. However, now in 2012, I'm just getting some of my memory back. I still have nightmares about this. I would never recommend something which nearly permanently destroyed me as a treatment.

In my first book Snappy But Happy which is a must-read for all the family, I related how when I was given E.C.T., I was given a general anaesthetic and a surge of electrical current was passed to my brain to cause a fit. It's supposed to alleviate depression; I vividly remember having about eight shock treatments while I was in hospital. It didn't work for me. It has caused me long term memory loss. E.C.T. isn't used very often now like it was some years ago. However, some people still do find that it helps them, and find it beneficial. There are other supporters you can have on your mental health team such as psychiatrists or mental health officials.

I am currently in remission from this terrible illness. I hope it stays that way. I attend a couple of drop-in groups for the mentally ill. Some drop-in centres or hospitals teach different skills. So whilst you're ill you can carry on learning whilst in hospital. You can learn art, pottery, cookery or go on trips out.

When someone is having a manic episode it is quite distressing to others around you. Some people with Bipolar find it difficult to trust other people, they tend to cut themselves off from the outside world. If you experience such feelings then you can talk to a G.P., psychiatrist, carer, family member or supportive friend.

You need to learn how to cope with being Bipolar. However, this is easier said than done. You need to develop a positive mental attitude and then you can achieve anything. Find out as much as you can about your condition and try to develop skills in order to control a mood swing. When you've achieved this goal you're halfway there.

There are certain things you can do to help yourself, and that includes taking regular exercise and eating the right foods. Try keeping a mood diary and when you are on a downer try to find ways of improving your mood.

If you can learn to help yourself you won't be relying on others too much and will have more control of your life. If you apply this method it can lead to greater self-confidence and lessen the chance of a relapse. Apart from exercise, good nutritious food will aid your recovery.

I have recently started exercise classes with my new husband Pete. The gym instructor doesn't pressure you into doing things you don't want to do. We have both so far benefitted from the programme. If we continue to keep to the plan we will achieve our goal of being fitter and continued weight loss. It's all about living a balanced life, eating fresh fruit and vegetables and regular exercise of course.

However, recovery isn't always a direct journey between being really ill and being really well. Some people find that they improve over a period of time, but then they may have small or large relapses. The important thing is not to give up on a positive attitude and believe that one day you will be well, and try not to get upset if you have a relapse, it's all part of the journey.

CHAPTER 11

HOW CAN YOU KEEP WELL AND WHAT DOES THE FUTURE HOLD FOR BIPOLAR SUFFERERS?

In order to stay well, content and happy in life you need to make certain lifestyle changes, sometimes these only need to be small changes rather than drastic changes. This includes remembering to take your medication as prescribed, and having plenty of sleep. If you aren't a heavy sleeper just set yourself a time for bed, go to bed and listen to a relaxation tape, this usually does the trick.

However, some people find that they have to adopt severe lifestyle changes, such as adopt a quieter lifestyle. Stress can affect your lifestyle so keep it to a minimum. Take time out for yourself, have a day where you just focus on yourself. Don't make drastic lifestyle changes on the spur of the moment, for example, give up your job or end a relationship, you may not be thinking clearly like you would if you were well. Just because you're feeling great, it doesn't mean that you don't need to keep an eye on your Bipolar. Keep taking your medication and seeing your G.P. regularly can help you stay in tip-top condition. Start enjoying life again.

Some people who are Bipolar enjoy talking to people on the internet who also have Bipolar, sharing experiences to comfort others and to make new friends. It is surprising to note that there are people out there who have the same condition.

Please bear in mind though, that some strategies of coping don't suit everyone. Some people find their own way of coping with the illness.

It's good to set goals that are achievable, for example "I plan to exercise at least twice a week for a period of one hour". This is a realistic goal that can be achieved. It's best to start with a goal that is small, rather than a goal that may never be obtainable. Your first goal may be to get your mood swings under control before you attempt another goal. Finding things that you really enjoy will help you cope with your illness.

I have found writing to be very therapeutic and has helped me get better. In the past couple of months, I have started to feel better in myself and want to share my thoughts and feelings with everyone. I feel really good within myself. Writing has given me a reason to live, as well as my beautiful daughter who has helped me get over the stressful and horrible illness that Bipolar is.

You need to learn to manage stress in your life. Everybody gets stressed; it's a part of life. Some people think that by drowning their sorrows, by drinking alcohol, it will help them, but in the long run, this only makes matters worse. Stress is a part of everyday life, however, it can be managed.

Regular sleep can help stress, and so can doing things that relax the body and mind. I find music or relaxation tapes very beneficial and stress-free.

When you want to achieve a goal in life, tread very carefully, take one step at a time and you will achieve your goal.

Some people find that prayer helps them spiritually and gives relief from stress, because God understands us better than we do ourselves and can help us. In order to keep and stay well continue to take all your medication as prescribed. Get plenty of sleep.

In order to maintain a healthy lifestyle, you need to do the following:

1) Take care of yourself
2) Take time out for yourself.
3) Keep up your social calendar. 4) Eat regular meals.
4) Have plenty of sleep.
5) Join a MIND group or other support group which focuses on the mentally ill. 7) Keep in contact with your G.P. or therapist.
6) Try and join a social drop-in group for people experiencing poor mental health. I met my new husband there, and have made lots of friends.

There are other ways of coping with the illness such as:

1) Do things together as a family – it's important that you keep the lines of communication open.

2) Be supportive to the person that has Bipolar Disorder.

3) There are ways to cope with the illness by firstly knowing about your illness, doing research, getting to know yourself better, the causes, treatments, coming to terms with the illness and accepting that it's part of you, then you will find it more manageable and easier to bare.

How can you keep in a positive mood?

1) Do enjoyable work and enjoyable hobbies. 2) Don't compare yourself to other people.

2) Always be helpful and considerate to other people. 4) Be positive.

3) Spend time with people that are supportive and helpful. 6) Look at your good points, not bad points in life.

If you are still feeling depressed, anxious or stressed seek out medical advice IMMEDIATELY for support, don't try to tackle this problem alone, G.P., psychiatrists, or therapists are there to help you. You may also find self-help groups to help with your depression, anxiousness or stress.

Self-esteem plays a significant part in your life. If you don't believe in yourself you will find life rather unbearable. You can change the way you feel; only you can do this.

Mind Info line is very helpful as are the Samaritans. What does the future hold for Bipolar sufferers? The future looks good for Bipolar sufferers In fact "The secret life of the manic depressive", was televised over the UK. This documentary was watched by some three million people. There were also 100,000 people who attended the BBCs' health website on Bipolar Disorder. New research has been discovered at universities such as Edinburgh, Manchester, Birmingham, Lancaster and Cardiff.

Today more people than ever are gaining control of Bipolar Disorder and living fruitful lives.

A professor from Cardiff university said "Over the coming years treatment will improve, prediction will improve and understanding will improve. Being diagnosed with Bipolar will be different for people of our children's generation compared to people of our parent's generation."

Ian Hulatt mental health advisor said," We are in the middle of a transition from institutional care to more family-based home care. We've still got a long way to go, but eventually, it will be recognised that the family is essential in maintaining the health of the individual."

Also, a lecturer in clinical psychology at Manchester University said"," Psychological support will be offered to everyone with Bipolar Disorder in the future.
There will also be more focus on learning skills to help relapse."

These are just a few examples of a professor, mental health advisor and lecturer of Bipolar Disorder. You have now come to the end of my part of the book, in the next chapter you will read about other peoples' experiences of mental distress. Also, my husband has written a chapter on What's life like living with Lorna? Also, there will be more poetry from the whole family and a few stories from my daughter.

I hope you find my book informative, useful and inspirational. If you follow the guidelines that I've written in the book you too will cope better with Bipolar and lead a more balanced life. Always remember that your G.P, Therapist, family and friends are there to support you.

When someone is depressed, inspired and manic, inspired is when you think you can do anything whereas when you are manic you know you can do anything.

At the end of the day getting better is mostly down to you, so don't forget to keep a positive mental attitude.

CHAPTER 12

EXPERIENCES OF PEOPLE WHO SUFFER FROM MENTAL ILLNESSES

BRIAN'S EXPERIENCE (I call him Brian for the sake of anonymity)

Brian was born in 1957 in Leicestershire. He is now 54. Before Brian got sick he used to hold down a really steady job at Desford Tubes. He enjoyed his work and he was happily married to Lynn. He used to have a cat called Ginger too. He'd look after the old folk in the village, putting the bins out. Brian down to this day is a very religious man. He suffered 2 break-downs and spent a lot of time in hospital and his marriage broke up in the process.

He was in and out of the old Carlton Hayes hospital and also the Bradgate mental health unit. During this time, he lost most of his friends. He lost all his confidence and didn't want to go out and spent time at home with mum and dad.

During recovery his religious faith helped him tremendously and he started going out more and mixing with people, he helped out at local football and cricket teams. He wanted to become a member of society once again. Although he still had bad nerves and wasn't eating properly, he prayed to God for help. He started to feel better and didn't have to rely on mum and dad so they didn't have to worry so much about their son.

Brian had never learnt to read well at school and during recovery, the local adult education officer helped teach Brian to read over a period of time at the drop-in centre. Brian didn't like travelling on buses and had taxis everywhere but had recovered to the extent that he started to travel on buses again and gained confidence to even go on holiday on his own by coach.

During recovery, Brian started once again to help village old folk by putting their bins out and by doing shopping for them. He now feels so well, he feels life is now brilliant and can look after himself and others. He now lives independently and doesn't rely on his parents, so they don't worry so much. In his own words, he has come a long way but his recovery has taken many years. Brian attends both a chapel and a church and firmly believes that his faith has helped him a lot.

PHILS'EXPERIENCE

(I call him Phil as this is to keep his anonymity)

"Grosse Seelen dulden still" – "great souls suffer in silence" (Schiller 1759 – 1805 from Don Carlos)

Phil is 58 at the time of writing. Phil was born in Leicestershire in 1954. Phil's mother was mentally ill for years after Phil's birth and had several stays in the old Carlton Hayes Mental Hospital.

Phil had a problem with bedwetting until he was six years old and had to see a specialist at Leicester Royal Infirmary. Other than that Phil was happy at home with his mum, dad and elder brother. He could read well - even before he started school, where he did well and was always first to volunteer to read out loud in class. He was a real extrovert, always first to climb a tree or swing over a stream on a rope.

Phil's life changed when at 8 years of age he was dragged into an outbuilding and raped by a stranger. Phil was physically scared (by having his trousers and underpants pulled down) but didn't know what was actually happening with the rape – although it felt very uncomfortable. What really scared and scarred Phil was when the rapist told him that if Phil told anyone about it – then the rapist would come back and murder him. Phil was 8 years old and believed him and was literally scared out of his wits– Phil stayed awake all that night – too frightened to sleep in case he was murdered or raped again. He changed overnight from being a brave extrovert into a cowardly introvert, who only wanted to hide himself from everyone and now hated to be put in the limelight.

It may seem impossible to believe but Phil was left in such a state of shock that even when he was older Phil's physical perception of himself was such that up to the age of forty, 6 feet tall and weighing 20 stone, he still felt he was only physically the same size as when he was eight. He would feel physically threatened by children 10 and over as well as adults. At sport he never followed through if throwing, bowling or playing golf – he found his mind restricted him to his 8-year-old physical size. He learnt to play snooker fairly well, but to this day uses a child's bridge length and back swing – he has never been able to retrain himself out of this habit.

Phil never told anyone, not even his mum or dad what had happened. He did hint at it to one person when he was 35. He did tell a psychiatrist at the age of 40 but no connections were made. For many years from the age of 8 until he was 55 he would have 2 or 3 nightmares a week – one was about a snake – years later Phil realised that the snake was a phallic symbol and represented the penis with which he had been violated. It wasn't until he was 51 years of age that his rape counsellor also pointed out that as some snakes are poisonous that this also alluded to the murder threat. The other set of nightmares were about being safe and happy in a group of people – then being singled out, chased, caught and murdered. Up to 3 years ago neighbours would be banging on Phil's door in the early hours of the morning to wake him up because he was shouting and screaming and making too much noise while reliving the rape or murder threat in his nightmares.

So from the age of 8, Phil suffered nightmares and was frozen emotionally. He didn't communicate his feelings at all – not even to his mum and dad, and never told them that he had been raped. Sometimes his mum would ask if he had had a good day at school, and Phil would always say yes he had had a good day – even if he had been beaten up by three bullies. Phil became very timid and cowardly, and couldn't speak up or stand up for himself – one day when he was 18 he was in a queue and a large lady stepped back and stood on Phil's foot – it hurt but Phil didn't have the confidence to ask her to move. For a long time, Phil was outwardly just a shell – a "non-person".

Phil was constantly frightened, every time he went out he was in a constant state of alertness – he couldn't relax, later in life he developed a ritualistic routine – because it felt "safe". Phil hated trying new activities, meeting new people or going to unfamiliar places. Also because of the rape Phil feared undressing in public. He loathed and dreaded the weekly shower after games at school – he always felt humiliated and re-violated.

Phil was reasonably clever and made it to grammar school, but being emotionally frozen had no ambition at all – he did well in the subjects he liked, but didn't try hard enough at the other subjects – he didn't realise their importance in "getting on". He left school with 1 "A" level and 6 "O" levels - quite an achievement considering his handicap – but how much better could he have done if he had applied himself – maybe he could have gone to university had his life not been ruined when he was 8.

In later life, Phil developed a "seat" phobia – in public places he hated being trapped in a row of seats with no "escape route" – at college, at church or in the theatre or cinema, and always tried to have an outside seat. When Phil was 16 he was trapped in a row of seats during a free period at school and was molested by an elder boy – (during this assault Phil was frozen with fear after what had happened when he was 8, and couldn't speak, shout out or defend himself) so put his "seat" phobia down to this experience. It wasn't until Phil was 49 and attending a phobia course that he remembered that his rapist worked in one of the local cinemas. Phil used to go to this cinema every Saturday from childhood till his mid-twenties – so whilst sitting in a row of seats Phil must have been subconsciously terrified that he would be raped again or murdered – hence the "seat" phobia.

When Phil left school he got a job in an office but had no ambition. At home, he learnt how to do things, but being emotionally frozen he never asked why? Phil had to be prompted by his mum and dad to bathe, change his clothes, clean his teeth, get his hair cut etc., etc., etc..

Phil might have been able to get away with appearing to cope with life but further tragedy struck when his mum died overnight at home when Phil was 23. Grief-stricken at losing his wife, Phil's father gave up on life and after a series of strokes died in hospital at 5.30am the day after Phil's 24th birthday.

Phil was now alone with no parents to prompt him to do things – so he didn't wash, bathe or change his clothes regularly and really smelt. He coped by drinking to excess most nights, although he had companions and a few friends he couldn't communicate his feelings to them – a few hinted that he needed to "sort himself out" but because Phil didn't know why he was like this and couldn't speak up things carried on like this for years. Phil never developed emotionally and despite falling in love with a few women never had the confidence to ask one out, let alone say that he was in love. (In fact, Phil didn't have his first adult sexual experience until he was 39 – even then he didn't make the first move, and unfortunately also confused sex with love.) Phil was starting to feel that life was like a continuous boxing match in which Phil would come out from his corner – his opponent would punch him below the belt, and what made it worse the referee did nothing, so Phil just had to carry on. So on with the next round – punched below the belt again – the ref did nothing again. This was how Phil felt every day for years – no small wonder that Phil developed depression and at times subconsciously didn't want to carry on this unfair contest and just wanted to lie on the canvas and be carried away to somewhere safe.

Phil went through the motions of being alive for about 10 years – coping by drinking, evading personal questions and not letting visitors into his house. Towards the end of this period, Phil was so scared of bumping into one of his neighbours that he stopped going outside to put rubbish in the dustbin. His house filled with 2 years of refuse and was becoming uninhabitable. He had used 1 coal fire – but his dad had organised this, so Phil ran out of coal after 2 years and didn't have the "voice" to phone to arrange more deliveries. Phil resorted to a tiny electric fire for heating. During the conversion to natural gas, Phil's gas service needed changing – but Phil didn't have the "voice" to ring up about it – so lost the gas supply to his cooker and water heating. Phil brought a one ring camping gas stove on which he cooked all his meals (tinned mainly) and boiled his hot water for cuppas, cooking, and washing. Phil was having a terrible life but was still unable to ask anyone for help.

It was 1991, with the build up of 2 years refuse Phil discovered that he was infested with mice, but he was still living in the house and suffering in silence. Then another neighbour complained about mice and the council sent a letter wanting to inspect Phil's house. Phil couldn't face the humiliation of letting anyone see how he lived, couldn't cope, couldn't ask for help and couldn't see a "way out".

Phil decided his only "way out" was to kill himself – so on his first suicide attempt Phil swallowed 78 paracetamols – he wanted to make sure. Within half an hour Phil vomited them all back up. He tried taking overdoses a further four times in five days – but each time Phil vomited them back up – he never sought medical attention or advice. Phil was at his wits end; he couldn't cope with his situation, had tried suicide 5 times and failed – what on earth could he do now?

So Phil resigned from his job, posted his house keys to his brother and at the age of 37 (going on 9) Phil ran away from home. Phil spent a week in London and a week in Skegness and then his money ran out. Phil rang the council who told him his brother and uncle were clearing the house so the council could get in and kill the mice. Phil returned home saw his GP who prescribed antidepressants and sleeping pills, and gave Phil a sick note with anxiety/depression written on it – which Phil read on the way out of the surgery, Phil wondered why the term anxiety was used because he didn't think he was anxious. However the doctor in his brief 10 minutes hadn't time to explain anything, nor was Phil given any leaflets on the subject (in contrast to when he was diagnosed diabetic) which might have given him some peace of mind. Nor did Phil know why all this had happened to him or why he couldn't function properly.

Just before this happened Phil had changed jobs from Accounts (which was very quiet with little contact with anyone at all – let alone customers!) to customer service – dealing with members of the public all the time. He had been bullied at work by a boss (1973 – 1985) and later bullied by other bosses (1990-1993). He had found this change difficult to deal with.

With a Grant from the council Phil's house was sorted out, refurbished with a rewire, shower, and gas central heating. He also had the house redecorated, brought new carpets and new furniture.

However, he was still timid and so stressed out by his new job that in total he took four periods off sick with depression in two years. He had seen a psychiatrist but had been discharged.

During his last period of time off from work, he discovered he had Type 2 diabetes – in the space of two months, the only two people he knew who had diabetes had both died with complications associated with diabetes. This made him even more depressed. Then Phil's boss's boss came out to see him – he could either face the sack for his poor sick record – or take voluntary redundancy at 39 with his pension starting at 50. Phil should have asked the Trade Union for advice and would probably have been given his pension on leaving on the grounds of ill health – but you guessed it - he didn't have the "voice" to ask for help. Since Phil owed £19,000 for the recent home improvements he would have to take the voluntary redundancy to keep his house.

Phil was told he couldn't be offered redundancy while he was off sick – so browbeat his GP to reluctantly sign him off. Phil had heard of cases where people were offered redundancy on Monday – and had left the same week. Phil expected this to happen to him – in fact by the end of the first week no one had even spoken to him about redundancy until his friend Hazel complained to the manager. Phil was then told that there was no money left for any more redundancies until the new Financial Year – three months away! During the 8 days since he had started back at work, he had had a total of 18 hours sleep, was exhausted and mentally distressed.

He couldn't cope again – if he went sick again he couldn't be offered redundancy and might be sacked and left with nothing – yet going to work was making him worse!

Phil had been a regular churchgoer but had stopped going five years earlier. That weekend he couldn't cope and collapsed on the floor and prayed "Lord Jesus please pray for me". Phil instantly leapt up into the air and was filled with energy and a positive frame of mind. During this period with little sleep, Phil went through a series of nightmares, remembered about the rape at eight and began to understand the ways in which it had affected his whole life so far – some of which has already been described.

Two days after the miracle healing Phil saw a blind man on the other side of the road about to walk into some scaffolding and shouted "look out" and stopped the blind man. Three days earlier Phil would have mumbled "look out" – but not loud enough for anyone to hear! Phil had found his "voice" and after being silent for 32 years now became a real chatterbox. During this period Phil was discussing what was happening and being supported by his local vicar and his friend at work Hazel – without their help Phil would have been unable to cope and is certain that he would have committed suicide...

Phil was healed in so far as he was able to go to work (under special terms – he could go home if he was ill) for a further five months till his redundancy offer came through and he was unemployed.

Within a few weeks of the miracle healing Phil had his first adult sexual relationship – even then he hadn't made the first move. Phil was worried by everything that was going on and wondered if he had worked everything out correctly. He went on a waiting list to see the psychiatrist but after three months no appointment had arrived. Phil rang the psychiatrist's secretary who told him an appointment was "in the post" for two months time! Phil asked if he did private work and if so when could he see him. The psychiatrist did do private work and could see him on the next working day for a fee of 100 guineas! Phil made the appointment and the psychiatrist told Phil he had worked everything out correctly and to keep the NHS appointment in two months time. Unfortunately, the psychiatrist never put the important information about the rape in Phil's NHS notes and never thought to test Phil for Post Traumatic Stress Disorder!

Phil was now 40, made redundant and put on Job Seekers Allowance – this lasted 3 months. Phil thought it had just been the pressure of his new job that had made him ill & after a short break he would be able to return to work – but he was still not sleeping having nightmares, flashbacks to the rape, feeling depressed and nervous. His GP put Phil back on the sick.

Around this time Phil developed severe agoraphobia – which is a fear of open OR public places. He had started feeling nervous travelling to and from work on the bus. Now Phil didn't have the confidence or nerve to be seen in public. He used to dash round to the corner shop at 7 am when everyone else was in a rush, and therefore would not have time to speak. His diet was consisting of cereal, toast, bacon and egg, bread, crisps and biscuits – not very healthy for a diabetic! He did manage a big shop about once a fortnight when he would stock up tinned food as he didn't have a freezer.

When Phil returned from the corner shop he had breakfast and looked at the paper, partly to look at the racing page – he would pick some horses out to back – but rarely got out to put the bets on – and the horses usually won. Fed up with this Phil opened a telephone account with a bookmaker so as not to miss out.

So Phil used to stay in with the curtains drawn so he couldn't be seen and hardly answered the door. Every day he tried to go out – but at the thought, his muscles went rigid and he stayed trapped in his armchair.

When Phil did venture out he experienced fear, hyperventilation, dizziness, collywobbles in the stomach, an urgent need to pee, and distorted vision – the pavement always seemed to be at an angle of 30 degrees. All this made it harder and harder each and every time he tried to get out, and every time he did actually make it out. He was lucky that a friend would pick him up and drop him home for a couple of hours of snooker every Friday night.

Phil attended one phobia course for ten weeks but couldn't put the techniques into practice. All this fear, inactivity and social isolation on top of depression made him feel suicidal for long periods of time. Fortunately, Phil was referred to a mental health social drop-in which he eventually attended 4 times a week and over a period made some very close friends – the drop-in was a lifeline – literally – Phil believes he would have attempted suicide if hadn't been for the drop-in centre.

Phil was still having panic attacks when he was out. Members of the public didn't help when some of them insulted him for being fat, and some people who knew him insulted him for being on the sick because "they could see nothing wrong with him" – well you can't see a mental illness, can you?

After three years at the drop in Phil went on another phobia course which helped a lot. Phil was taught to control his symptoms by slowing his breathing down, challenging illogical thoughts, and undertaking regular relaxation exercises.

Phil gained in confidence and thought he was feeling a lot better (really he was actually just coping - with a life spent "ticking over"). He got involved in a mental health service user group that aimed to improve the local mental health services.

Phil managed to help with the local group for six years as secretary – during this time the local group had some interesting guest speakers including the local M.P. (twice), and the Acting Medical Director of Mental Health Services for Leicestershire Partnership Trust. He also got involved at county level three times for about 4-6 months. Each time the stress of travel, going to meetings that took 5 hours when the travel was included, and having 3 –
6 meetings a month made Phil ill. Phil knew he was stressed – but didn't realise how much until he vomited while waiting to catch a bus to a meeting. He, therefore, was not able to be an active member of these groups and had to resign on health grounds.

In 2006 Phil started using a voluntary counselling service to deal with the rape – (which he had mentioned to 3 NHS staff – but was ignored as it happened too long ago!). At the end of the 2nd session for homework, he was asked to write a notional letter to the rapist telling him what he had done and how it had affected and ruined Phil's life. During the writing of this 6 page A4 letter, Phil had to go and vomit 3 separate times – delayed shock starting to wear off after 44 years! Through the letter and later counselling Phil was able to face and talk about the rape itself and all its later psychological knock-on effects - he could have had a closer relationship with his parents, done better at school, maybe gone to university, been open with friends, kept himself and his house clean and tidy, had a good job, gone on holidays, had girlfriends, maybe got married and had children etc., etc. etc.. What a happy alternative life he could have had – had it not been for the rapist.

Phil was now feeling well – as in just ticking over – as long as he wasn't exposed to too much stress. Phil felt and still feels that he wouldn't be able to cope with returning to work – last time he had to have 4 periods of sickness with anxiety/depression – and couldn't cope with 4 half days a month when he was in the mental health service user group. He'd only had the confidence to go on 1 holiday in 34 years but was now able to enjoy holidays with friends.

Phil still attends a local mental health social drop-in where he has made many lifelong "real" friends who have helped with physical tasks (like moving house) and been a source of support. He was smitten by a lady from the drop-in, in 2002 but they broke up. In 2009 they started to see each other, got engaged and married in 2010.

In 2009 Phil started to see a private psychotherapist who within two appointments discovered that Phil was suffering from Post Traumatic Stress Disorder as a result of the rape, being molested, and the shock of the overnight death of his mother.

Phil has 1 "A" level (in history), 6 "O" levels, O.N.C. (BTEC) & H.N.C. in business studies. Phil has many hobbies and interests – old films, military history, classical music, horse racing, playing and watching snooker, real ale beer festivals, looking at art, and watching drama – especially Tennessee Williams, Terrence Rattigan, and Shakespeare (he saw The Merchant of Venice at the Globe Theatre in London in 2008). He also dabbles in creative writing – poetry, short stories, he has plans for a Television play set in the Great War, a comedy play and two books – one a detective story, the other a Second World War thriller set in the Mediterranean. After 45 years of silent suffering his original extrovert character has re-emerged – he has compiled and hosted several quiz nights, and has been able to perform at Christmas parties with impressions of Tommy Cooper, George Burns, Harold Wilson, John Wayne, and as Laurel and Hardy singing "on the Blue Ridge Mountains of Virginia". On holiday when staying in small hotels he has also done some stand-up comedy (when there was no other entertainment provided) on one occasion he was actually paid by the owner – a single brandy (it took two doubles to actually get on stage) – despite all the tragedies in his life, Phil has a wicked sense of humour!

Phil is still on antidepressants but no longer sees a psychiatrist. Phil did experience suicidal feelings in 2011 when he was struggling to cope as a recently married husband after 35 years living alone.

You wouldn't think that it was possible that 1 isolated event – being in the wrong place, at the wrong time, with the wrong person could have such an adverse knock-on effect on almost every area of Phil's personality, mental state, career, sex life – in fact, whole life.

Phil's ongoing journey of recovery has been a long, slow, painful and distressing experience (including many months of suicidal thoughts over many years) and has taken 50 years so far – almost a lifetime. After all these years of tragedy, wasted life, and wasted opportunity (through no fault of his own) Phil feels that "life" owes him something, and is, at last, receiving some measure of happiness in his recent marriage.

The rules of the UK's benefit system have changed recently – people on the old Incapacity Benefit are being asked how their illness affects their ability to work – if you don't achieve the necessary points you can be put in the Work-Related Activity Group – with a view to going on to Job Seekers Allowance; with the humiliation of "signing on" every fortnight and applying for jobs – if there are any, - then feeling a failure if you aren't offered a job because of your age and mental health history. Also, Phil is afraid of returning to work because he felt bullied by four previous supervisors, and couldn't cope with that again. In 2013 Phil received his "limited capability for work" questionnaire – his problem – he can't put all his past experiences on the form – and how can he explain all this in a face to face interview. Thanks a lot, just when Phil thought he was getting some enjoyment out of life at last - this happens – Phil's depression has got worse, he is experiencing really poor quality sleep patterns and insomnia with the worry, and is now experiencing some erectile dysfunction, his blood pressure has gone from 125/83 to 175/102, and when he walks outside the house he feels like half his brain is missing & the other half is set in concrete, he also feels like he is bearing a 1 cwt bag of coal on his shoulders, and also feels like he has a ten-inch thick iron girdle around his chest. Phil feels this ordeal has put him back by eight years. He is now having regular suicidal thoughts about the whole process – but Phil feels that if he does commit suicide the government will have succeeded in moving 1 more person off benefits. So much for the phrase, "Salus populi suprema lex esto!" – "let the welfare of the people be the final law!" – (Cicero 106-43 bc from De Legibus).

Phil puts his recovery down to : a self-realization (in 1994) as to how his being raped at eight had affected his whole life; his belief in God and the power of prayer (especially by his friend Dave); the support of his friend from work and Guardian Angel Hazel and of his local vicar (1994); 20 years of medication; volunteer rape counselling (2006-7); the support and friendship of members of the local mental health drop-in centre (2000-2013); and the treatment, advice and support of his psychotherapist/hypnotherapist Sally (2009/13). Phil has also learnt to endure the really dreadful days of depression/suicidal thoughts - because sometime in the future you will feel better; to be content on a "ticking over" day – just do what you can; and to really enjoy and get the most out of the occasional good day.

Phil's hopes for the future are to stay as mentally and physically well as possible; to love, care for and support his wife; to pursue his creative writing projects; and to see some of the places he never had a chance to see before – Paris, Florence, Rome, Sorrento (achieved in 2013!), Egypt and Hastings! '

LYDIA'S EXPERIENCE (From her own perspective)

To begin my story we start from the year 1999. When I was born, and throughout my first few years, my mum spent a lot of time in the hospital. Which was the start of her struggle with mental illness. Around the first year after my birth, my Mum and Dad split up. This meant that during my childhood, I went backwards and forwards between the two. As my dad had main custody of me, I would spend the week and then stay at my mum's at the weekend. In my early years, I would be looked after at the local nursery while dad worked in the day. There was a lot of help in looking after me, by my auntie, grandma and a few family friends. When I started school, I would be picked up by the nursery staff and spend the rest of the day at the nursery till Dad was able to pick me up. Then in 2006 things began to change.

Dad started a new relationship with Jackie, who later in 2007 officially became my stepmom when she and Dad married in February that year. My first memories of her were her babysitting me while Dad attended his cousin's wedding. I remember a mousetrap going off and scaring us both half to death. And a few times I stayed overnight at her house. We'd play games and she'd take me out and about, including to Mcdonalds which was always such a treat. There was even a time when we were sorting my bed for the night, that I sat on the mattress at the top of the stairs and slid down on it. It was great. I got used to having her around pretty quickly and was super excited to be a bridesmaid. But it was still a big change in my life.

I loved spending time at both Mum's and Dad's houses, but things were very different in each house. At Dad's things were fairly strict, whilst at mums, it was way more relaxed. Which did create some confusion along the way. And while I had more freedom at Mum's there was much more responsibility. For starters, I essentially became mum's carer while I was there. I remember fetching drinks, meals, sorting her medication for her, doing various chores for her and even bathing her. Mum struggled financially sometimes and there was a point where we had no hot water so I was told to run backwards and forwards with the kettle, in order to fill up the bath for her. There was also taking care of whatever pet she had at the time which was mainly cats.

That's not to say I didn't get time to be a kid, truthfully I did and too much in fact. Because of her bipolar, Mum often spent many hours of the day in bed, sometimes not coming down till tea-time so I was often left to my own devices. Which either was TV or gaming on the computer. (Gaming lead to an unhealthy addiction and got me into a lot of trouble a few years later)

Flash forward to 2010 when Mum got married to Pete. That was a whole other thing for me to get used to. One of my first memories meeting him was at the mental health group he and mum used to go to. I remember a discussion going on and something mentioned about flyers. I looked over and saw Pete flapping a piece of paper like it was a bird, it was quite funny. He has such a funny sense of humour, always cracking jokes and doing impressions. Mum took me with her quite a few times, most likely because I was still a little too young to be left alone. Then I found out they were getting married and I got to be a bridesmaid again! Pete did a lot for mum which meant that I could be a kid more now, rather than a carer.

Then peaked my preteen and early teenage years. Going through puberty is rough, but at the same time, lots of other things were happening. At school, I started getting bullied by a boy in my class. But all the while I was told that old saying 'boys will be boys' and especially the "He's only mean to you because he likes you,". There are so many things wrong with those statements. Why? Because it's essentially condoning emotional and psychological abuse! And especially abuse towards girls and women! Which isn't okay!

The bullying consisted of mainly name-calling though there was some physical bullying as well. Like being pushed down the stairs all the while, being pushed around, having things thrown at me, (Sewing needles, snowballs with stones and other various items). There was even a particular incident where the bully grabbed the chair I was sitting on, dragged it across the floor and tried to push me out of it, even kicking me a few times. It shook me up a hell of a lot. Truthfully one of the worst things about the bullying is that everyone in my class knew it was going on but did nothing. Half of them found it funny, some people joined in while others stayed quiet, almost like they were pretending not to notice. That incident with me being pushed out of a chair, some laughed but most turned on me after I told the teacher what was happening. Rumours went around that I'd said he kicked and punched me. I explained several times that it wasn't true but he did kick me. No one believed me and to this day I think that it affected how everyone viewed me. I was given dirty looks and no one really spoke to me.

Being a bystander is just as bad as being a bully because you're essentially saying that the bully's behaviour is okay, that you're okay with seeing someone in distress, someone being physically and verbally abused. Because you're standing there letting it happen when you could be doing something to help! If you're able to, you should always help if you can.

Statistically (as of 2018) nearly 1 in 5 students report being bullied during the school year, which means that bullying impacts more than 5 million youths per year. Bullying impacts their learning ability, sleep patterns, academic abilities and mental health. Causing issues with low self-esteem, depression, anxiety and sometimes family problems. Students that experience bullying or cyberbullying are two times more likely to attempt suicide. Approximately 1 in 20 experience a suicide in a single year. This makes suicide the 2nd leading cause of death for individuals aged 10-34

But thankfully I'm not part of that last statistic. Though that doesn't mean that I haven't been affected in some way. My self-esteem was severely damaged and though I used to be a little shy around people, I became completely closed off and silent. I also struggled a lot more in social situations.

My friendships more often than not ended badly. Either they'd end up turning on me, never letting me have an opinion on anything, or I'd get forgotten about. It was always the same scenario. At first, it would be great! We'd talk all the time, hang out together, basically be inseparable. We'd always confide in each other and always be there for each other. But as time went on they'd stop putting in the effort. We'd rarely talk and I'd be the only one coming up with the plans which they'd constantly come up with excuse after excuse to avoid. When we did eventually meet up, they'd talk about all the things they'd done with other people, things WE had planned to do.

All of these failed friendships took a massive toll on my mental health and I slipped into the mindset that I was the problem. I wasn't good enough. In my mind, it made sense to me that the common factor in all my failed friendships was me. So it's my fault and I was a horrible person and friend. I even believed that I deserved to be alone.

Throughout my teenage years, things really kicked off between me and Jackie. We'd often argue over the slightest things (usually me picking fights about everything). I had all this inner anger inside of me that unfortunately got taken out on her. I know it mainly comes from a place of pain and anxiety (or if I'm worried or stressed about anything), but sometimes I wonder whether part of it has been learned from experiencing both parent's anger on multiple occasions.

Mum's couldn't always be helped as it's mostly down to her bipolar and if she's having an episode or having an off day she can get quite snappy very quickly. This often meant we also argued frequently. We could be like chalk and cheese sometimes. Mum often was unable to cope after arguments so Dad would be called to bring me back to his house. There were even some scary incidents where mum started repeatedly saying how bad of a mum she was and that we were better off without her. Sometimes she would threaten to pack a bag and leave but most times she'd threaten to kill herself. As a child, it was very scary and something that traumatised me, especially the one incident where she locked herself in the bathroom with her medication, threatening to take an overdose. Pete managed to coax her out eventually. But it was a terrifying experience and in those moments I felt so helpless. I'm honestly so thankful Pete was there otherwise I dread to think about what could have happened.

Dad's temper on the other hand was way different. More often than not you'd have to tiptoe around him because the slightest thing could set him off. He could yell and scream like a banshee. He'd slam doors violently and sometimes throw things. He once even ripped the front of a drawer right off with his bare hands! Needless to say, I was pretty scared of him, sometimes even terrified. I would often head off to the opposite side of the house, far away from him. It was also hard not to blame myself for it either, since every time he got set off, it always felt like it was because of me. Something I said or did. All I wanted was a bit of attention, a bit of love. Because honestly he never spent that much time with me.

It's crazy how one minute he could be perfectly fine. Completely loving, laughing and joking around but the next he's yelling and screaming. Sometimes it would happen out in public which was honestly humiliating. I've also never been one for conflict, even though I often ended up picking fights. But it's more of a defence mechanism to me. Like that fight or flight thing when you feel scared or threatened.

Dad's aggression and the bully from school (as it was a boy), both contributed towards some major trust issues with the opposite gender. There was another incident that contributed as well. In 2015 I was groomed online by a paedophile. It happened when I was on a video call with an online friend. (We'd spoken regularly on Twitter and video called a lot on skype so I knew she was who she claimed to be) We decided to use a different app called OOVOO one day, as skype wasn't working. While we were in a video call, the paedophile hacked into our call, joining it and flashing his genitals at us, doing very sexual things. We both turned our cameras off so he couldn't see us but he kept writing in the chat, saying what he would do for us if we put the cameras back on. He left the video call after a few seconds but kept jumping back in and out several times. The final time, after doing the same things as before, he began threatening us when we didn't comply. He kept saying he could see my friend through her window and would harm her if I didn't comply. It was very scary, but I still didn't put my camera back on and he eventually left us alone. This incident scarred me and diminished my trust in the opposite gender a whole lot more. Meaning I was always uncomfortable around anyone of the opposite gender and would refuse to talk to or see any health care professionals that were men.

The incident was dealt with by police but despite being a known paedophile, he got off with just community service. You should always be wary of who you're talking to online and never give out personal information. Only talk to people you actually know or have met in person.

Going back to home life, there was a lot of conflict, but despite all this, I still had school to deal with. My grades were usually pretty good despite everything, even the bullying. Which thankfully did eventually stop when Jackie was more forceful with the school and as a result, they finally did something after more than two years. At the beginning of my GCSE years, that's when things started to go downhill. The amount of stress and pressure I was put under was insane. There were several times I had panic attacks. (We were also the first ever GCSE year in our school so there was twice as much pressure.) My homework performance progressively got worse, especially with science. I really struggled with science, I just couldn't understand much of it, but somehow ended up in the top set which did Triple Science. (Which basically means you have three exams instead of the usual two, per each science. Biology, Physics and Chemistry) It also meant staying after school once or twice a week and even going to school during the holidays. It was also a lot more difficult. But most other subjects were alright. Then came exam time and the day before my music exam, the music teacher took me out of a lesson to tell me that I wasn't going to pass the exam because I wasn't as good as everyone else. I wasn't good enough. (Well the joke is on her because I did pass! It was D, the lowest passing grade. But still a pass!)

That is one of the things that hit me hard though, as music was one of my biggest passions. It's always been my dream to be a professional singer, but I never believed I was good enough. It wasn't until I started taking keyboard/piano lessons for the second time (I started in primary school but finished when I started high school.) as it was compulsory for the music GCSE. (Which I wasn't informed about till a quarter of the way through the course, so thanks teacher!) My piano teacher got me to sing a couple of lines from the song we were working on and then decided I was also going to sing the piece as well as play it on the piano. It was the first time I was told that I could sing and where my passion for music began to swiftly grow. Writing was another passion, which also coincides with my music passion because apart from writing stories, I also write songs. So as you can imagine, English was one of my favourite subjects aside from music. It was also my best subject. I was predicted A's.

When it came to getting my GCSE results, to say I was disappointed was an understatement. Especially with my English grades as I'd only got a C. And knowing that I could have done way better and was capable of doing better left me beyond gutted. I also mainly got Cs on everything else (Aside from two B grades but I didn't really take note of them at the time) I thought I was a disappointment to my parents and believed I was a failure. I was so upset and distraught that day, I did something I'm really not proud of. I cut myself.

This wouldn't be the last time. There have been many occasions where I've done it. As my mental health began to decline, the more I began to self-harm. It started with a small part of my wrist but then progressed to the whole of both forearms. Now I know what you might be wondering, did my parents know? No. But I told my grandma about it. She's always been my rock, been there for me through everything I've gone through. And she told my Dad. But after the conversation, I had with him and Jackie, I kept it to myself. I'm often prone to bottling things up and sometimes when I keep things in too long, I have a breakdown and sometimes I self-harm.

Why did I keep things to myself? Partly because I was ashamed and partly because I didn't think anyone would understand me. Or understand how much I was struggling. And also because I've been told several times that 'It's just a teenage thing'. Mental illness during adolescence is a very real thing. Half of all mental health conditions start by 14, although a lot of those cases go undetected, sadly. Statistically, adolescents have the highest rate of self-injurious behaviours.

Why do people self-harm? It can be for various reasons. But often it is related to specific experiences and can be a way of dealing with something that is happening in the moment or that has happened in the past. For me, it was a combination. In a way, it is a way of release from all the emotional pain. Some people become unable to cope with the emotional pain and use self-harm as a coping mechanism. Sometimes people do it because they want to try to feel something, often if they've been feeling mainly numb or empty. It is also done as a form of punishment to oneself if they are feeling immense guilt over something that has happened. Or if their mood is so low and they feel so nervous, they might believe that they deserve it.

All of the above are reasons why I did it. It continued for quite some time. Throughout the start of college I was harming myself regularly but always wore long sleeves to keep it covered, even on really hot days. Which was the same around the house. However, sometimes I wouldn't even try to hide the marks on my arms. But Dad and Jackie never really noticed. Even when it was right in front of them. There were a few times I deliberately had them visible because I wanted them to notice. I wanted them to know, to see how much I was struggling. It was like I was screaming out for help but no one could hear me.

College really didn't help me a lot. I decided to do a music course and it was such a great course. I was very anxious about starting because I was so scared I'd get bullied again. That I wouldn't fit in. I've never really fitted in anywhere, never felt like I belonged. Even within the religion, I was brought up in, that was the one place I especially didn't think I belonged, I always felt like such an outsider. But my fears were proved to be right. Once again I was getting bullied. This time, however, it was by the teacher.

Throughout my short time at college, the teacher, who I shall call Bob for this, tormented me a lot. We would work in groups for the practical work on the course. (Technically bands as we were all musicians). It was a really fun experience. We'd rehearse various songs a couple of times a week. We had a drummer, bassist, guitarist, pianist and two vocalists, (Me and a boy). The songs were mainly rock songs, suited to the male singer's vocals, so I struggled a lot. Bob sure didn't make things easy. Throughout rehearsals he would constantly play around with the microphones we were using, turning mine all the way up or all the way down. He'd also constantly harass me and get in my face as I was singing. (Now Bob was aware of my anxiety and the fact that my self-confidence was basically
non-existent. And looking back, I think he would've been aware of how his actions could have affected me.) This obviously meant that I was more exposed when I was singing and it made me more self-conscious and insecure about my singing. Afraid of being laughed at if I made a mistake or went off-key.

There wasn't an awful lot I could do, except stand there. Sometimes it would make me shut down completely. One particular incident affected me the worst. During the rehearsal, Bob was relentless, constantly turning my microphone volume up and down. He also repeatedly got in my face, trying to get me to sing louder. (Which, to point out, wasn't an issue as I could be heard just fine by everyone else, even over the live instruments). As a result, I stopped singing completely, only able to look at the floor. My body was physically shaking as I tried to hold back the tears. I felt so humiliated and embarrassed, especially as it was all in front of everyone else. As I slowly began to get used to college and the band, he tried removing me from the band, making me work at the technical things in the studio instead. His excuse was that it would be better for my anxiety. I protested because I love performing, in front of crowds I'm actually fine (Which he would have been known if he'd have given me a chance). But in smaller groups, it's more private and mess-ups are easier to pick up as you're way more exposed. Putting me in the non-performing group would not have helped me with my confidence or anxiety, it would have hindered me. Fortunately, though, I was kept with the performing group.

There also have been several instances where he yelled at me. And as someone who has grown up in situations where I've been repeatedly yelled at for things, you can imagine it would make me pretty fearful. One time I was off sick for just over a week with tonsillitis and the day I got back to college, he kept me back while everyone went on their morning break. Bob proceeded to lecture me about my lack of attendance, not believing that I was off sick the previous week, despite me having a note from the doctor. The one thing that baffled me was that he was more concerned about me allegedly lying to my Dad about going into college, (which 1. had nothing to do with him and 2. was a misunderstanding. I'd told dad I was going in on Monday, but on the actual day I still wasn't feeling 100% so I didn't go in.). He proceeded to yell and lecture me about lying to my Dad and also about my assignment which was late. (Because I was off sick so was unable to hand it in on time.)

When he finally let me go on my break, I left the room and burst into tears. As I left the music department, I hung around nearby because there was literally no time left for my break. I stood by the railing crying my eyes out and looked down at the floor below. (The way the floors were designed, in some areas you could see the floor below and the ground floor). As I stared down at the floor below, I contemplated climbing over the railings and jumping. I was so tired of the constant humiliation; I was tired of my parents not seeing how badly I was struggling. It made me wonder if they even cared, if they'd even miss me if I was gone. Maybe they'd be better off not having a disappointment of a daughter. I doubted why I had decided to do this music course when I was clearly awful at it. Completely worthless. But thankfully one of my classmates came over just at the right time, and asked if I was okay. I told them a little about what had happened and she consoled me. We then headed into class together.

My time at college ended up being rather short. Due to my anxiety and the bullying from my teacher, my attendance slipped down to around 52-56% and the college called my parents and I was given two weeks to improve it (meaning I had to be in every single day no matter what) otherwise I would lose my place on the course. Around this time, I began getting help from 'The Child and Adolescent Mental Health Service (aka CAMHS) because I'd finally been able to reach out to my parents and make them realise that I needed help. During the start of week one, we were called into a meeting with the college, but unfortunately, I was physically unwell and couldn't attend. Even if I was able to, I still would have been too scared to face them all, especially Bob. My Dad went in my place and when he returned he explained that as soon as they found out I was getting help for my anxiety, they kicked me straight off the course. (This is a discriminatory act and honestly kind of hypocritical of a college that claimed to be all-inclusive and against discrimination.). He also told me that Bob had acted way too nice, like he was covering up something. (Aka his bullying).

The college let me down and handled this situation very poorly. For starters, I was supposed to get a helper, who would be there to help me deal with my anxiety, but that never happened. Secondly, they never let me even try to redeem myself and kicked me out as soon as they found out I was getting help for my mental health issues. They also lied to my peers, claiming I'd simply decided to leave the course.

This essentially crippled my mental health, as afterwards my anxiety became so bad that I was unable to leave the house. Unable to go anywhere, especially alone. I couldn't pick up the phone and was barely able to speak to any healthcare professionals, always relying on Dad or Jackie to speak for me. I also kept getting panic attacks.

CAMHS can be a great help for the children and teenagers that are struggling and with their families to help them understand what their child is going through, but it isn't always the case. Like with my experience with CAMHS. After being assessed, I was referred to an anxiety group. There were four sessions with a small group of other young people and two leaders that helped us understand our anxiety and how to cope with it. Which was a good thing and that really did help. During this time, I did also get put on Sertraline for my anxiety and depression but this didn't last long as I didn't get on with it very well. Sometimes medication works for some people but it doesn't work for everyone.

While under CAMHS, I was also referred to another place in regards to my anxiety. The lady that I saw there wasn't very helpful and essentially told me to just snap out of it. Yes, that's right, a mental health professional told me to snap out of it! And during all of this, I was placed on a waiting list for therapy and counselling which I stayed on throughout my time with CAMHS. I was under them for about two years, until I was dropped because I was just about to turn 18.

We had some family therapy sessions as well while we were there, which did help me talk to them about things that I normally would hide away, so that is one thing that came from it. Aside from that, my mental health really wasn't addressed at all. I had been referred there due to self-harming but the only times it was addressed was to see if I had done it. Not to tackle why or exploring other methods of coping with things and helping me stop. Just if I had done it recently and at the time I was still doing it quite regularly. The one time when I hadn't for maybe just less than a month, they thought I was fine and nothing was wrong with me, even though I'd said I still was getting thoughts. But it was ignored.

I was also referred to this place called The Yes Project and given a mentor. She came with me to a few doctor appointments, including the one where the doctor referred me to the adult mental health service after I was discharged from CAMHS. I did a Nail Art course through the Prince's Trust and it was an amazing experience. The staff there were very understanding. The course itself was amazing as well and I learned a great deal about nails. Nail conditions, nail care, how to do manicures and also massages (Hand and arm). The best part was getting qualifications from it, which means I can get a job in a nail salon if I wish to. The Yes Project is designed to help young people get back into college or work and even start up their own businesses. However, I was not in the right place for this and was far from ready to get back to college or find a job. My experiences at college had made me fearful of ever going back on a course. I also still had my mental health to take care of first so my time with The Yes Project didn't last.

With the adult mental health service, things were very different. The assessment was more thorough and they delved into things that had happened in my childhood. We created action plans and there I was actually listened to. I also got sent to the job centre where I was assessed and it was determined that I would be put on ESA. This will obviously be until I am able to get into full-time work and have a steady income. Through the adult mental health service, I realised that it wasn't just a teenage thing. That it wasn't just nothing or all in my head or something to snap out of. I was diagnosed with Anxiety Disorder and Dysthymia (Also known as Persistent depressive disorder).

It was a long, rocky road with the mental health services. For years I never left the house, only for appointments. Most of my friends drifted away, so I never really had anyone to speak to. A lot of the time it was hard to feel anything. Whenever I did feel something it was always negative emotions. I lost interest in a lot of hobbies and passions and spent most of my days either watching the tv or playing games on my computer. More often than not, I'd see that people I used to know from school had jobs they loved, were studying at university, had great outings with their friends, had found love, some even had started to settle down and have kids of their own. I longed to find a fulfilling career, to have a lasting relationship and to settle down one day. But I often felt that no one would want me. That I had too many issues that no one would ever want to deal with. That I was too ugly and too worthless. And with my anxiety in overdrive, my life seemed to be permanently on hold.

But I gradually found ways of coping, one of which was through music. Sometimes when I couldn't make sense of everything that was going on in my head, or of all the emotions running through me, I often ended up finding a song that would describe it to a T. It is such a surreal feeling when you find a song you connect to so much! I also found I was able to express my emotions through songwriting and singing. Being creative really gets your mind working and you find yourself able to let go as your emotions pour out onto the page, whether it be through lyrics, poetry, stories, painting or other craftwork. Listening to music can also be very therapeutic and help you relax and destress. Exercise also helps a lot and though I am not the most active person, I do enjoy long walks and hikes, being out and close to nature. There are also a lot of groups that you can go to and meet people while you participate in various activities.

It's also important to have a good support network. While my Dad and Jackie have supported me and helped me get the help I need, the biggest support has been from my mum and my grandma on my dad's side. (Nana). Mum was always there to listen and she understood everything I was going through and shared some of her struggles with me which helped me understand that I wasn't alone. She gave me comforting hugs and let me say what I needed to say and gave me advice. Sometimes we'd pray together. While I'm not particularly religious now, and even back then had my doubts, it did prove to be a source of comfort. Nana has been my rock through everything that I've been through. She's like my lifeline at times, someone I can call no matter how late, and she will always be there to listen. She always gives me advice and reassures me a lot. She looked after me a lot for the first few years of my life, while mum was in hospital, which I think is why I have such a strong bond with her. She is the person I talk to the most. About anything. We always have a laugh together and you can easily see where I get my sense of humour from.

At the time of writing this, it is 2021. I have been volunteering at my local animal shelter which proves to be a great therapy for me, spending all that time with the animals. (Primarily cats and dogs, which studies have shown, petting or playing with a cat or dog, greatly reduces stress. It's even proven that owning one reduces the chances of having a stroke or heart attack. So pets are pretty great. They also provide great companionship). Working at the animal shelter also allows me to mix with people and socialize more. I recommend trying volunteering. There are a lot of different places to volunteer and it is a great way of mixing and getting used to people, as well as helping you find new interests and gaining work experience which will help you get a job in the future. It also gets you out of the house and out of bed in the morning.

I'm still not where I want to be yet, but I am gradually getting there. I was discharged from the mental health service a few years ago and while I believe it wasn't the correct decision as my issues with self-harm weren't fully addressed, I am using what I've learned from my time with them, using the techniques I've been shown. I have been clean for quite a while, but should I have any relapse, I am prepared to reach out and talk to my GP again to get the help that I need. I am working on getting back up on my feet, one bit at a time. I am honestly looking at the future with hope and excitement as I begin to resume my life again. Dealing with mental illnesses can be a very difficult and very long and tiring journey but if you take care of yourself: getting the help you need, finding the right support network, maintaining a healthy lifestyle and finding ways to keep your mind busy, through creativity and other things, you can get there!

One of the most important things I've learned is that you should never be afraid to ask for help. You may think asking for help makes you weak or less of a person but actually, it is one of the bravest things you can do. It takes a lot for one to admit that you're struggling. So never be afraid to ask! And be persistent too! Sometimes you may feel like you're not getting heard or people aren't taking you seriously, but never give up. Keep trying and keep pushing. Someone will hear you. Though it can be hard sometimes, never feel like you're alone, there are many people out there in the world who have experienced similar things and will understand what you've gone through. Some are closer to you than you think. *'Everyone, no matter how big and strong, could use a little help sometimes. Never be afraid to ask for help when you need it. What are we here for, if not for each other?'* - Doe Zantamata.

The last thing I'll say is that if you feel like you're behind everyone in life, you're not. Everyone goes through life at their own pace. *'You're not behind in life. There is no timetable that we all must follow. It's made up. 7 billion people can't do the same thing in the same order. What's early? What's late? Compared to who? Don't beat yourself up for where you are. It's YOUR schedule and everything is right on time.'* - Emily Maroutian.

So no matter where you are in life you can still get to where you want to be. There is no pressure to be in a certain place in your life and have certain things (career, relationships, kids) they will all come to you when the time is right. Take care of yourself and try to live your life to the fullest. Hold on through the tough and make the most of the good, appreciating every moment. *'I hope that in the year to come, you make mistakes. Because if you are making mistakes, then you are making new things, trying new things, learning, living, pushing yourself, changing yourself, changing your world. You're doing things you've never done before, and more importantly you're doing something. So that's my wish...Don't freeze, don't stop, don't worry that it isn't good enough, or it isn't perfect, whatever it is: art, or love, or work or family or life. Whatever it is you're scared of doing, do it. Make your mistakes, next year and forever.'* - Neil Gaiman

And don't be afraid to aim high! It is never too late to get up and try again. Or even chase your dreams. *'For what it's worth...it's never too late, or in my case too early, to be whoever you want to be. There's no time limit. Start whenever you want. You can change or stay the same. There are no rules...We can make the best or worst of it. I hope you can make the best of it. I hope you see things that startle you. I hope you feel things you've never felt before. I hope you meet people who have a different point of view. I hope you live a life you're proud of, and if you're not, I hope you have the courage to start over again.'* -F.Scott Fitzgerald

My dream is to be a singer, performing on the stage, and who knows? Maybe you'll see me in the charts one day!

CHAPTER 13

LIVING WITH LORNA

By Pete

"If you can fill the unforgiving minute, with sixty seconds worth of distance run" (from If by Rudyard Kipling 1865 – 1936).

What an amazing human being my lovely wife Lorna really is.

Lorna is a person who has to live with Bipolar Disorder, since we live together I also have to live with her Bipolar!

For a start I have never heard Lorna complain or question why she is one of the "One in One Hundred" who has been burdened with Bipolar – she just accepts it as part of her life.

When she is more stable, the medication makes her very tired – so she spends longer than the average person asleep or resting in bed. (I struggle to keep a fair share of our bed. For example, if I go to the bathroom for a pee in the wee hours, when I return I usually find Lorna trying to sleep diagonally – her legs are across my 40% of our bed.)

With the need for extra sleep or rest, Lorna on average only has the energy to go out about 3 times a week – to medical appointments, the West Leicestershire Mind mental health social drop-in group, her mums, her place of worship, her knit and natter group, the gym, or non-grocery shopping.

On an average day, she's probably at her best between 5pm and 11pm. Sometimes she can only function really well for perhaps 2 half days a week – and it's staggering the amount of tasks she can accomplish in the small space of time that she is limited to by her illness and medication. When Lorna is low she can only fill Kipling's "unforgiving minute (If)" with about 1 second worth of distance run, but when she's high she can fill that unforgiving minute with about 240 seconds worth of distance run! This just goes to show the astounding contrast between her high and low episodes in her Bipolar.

One thing I really love about Lorna is that even when she is feeling only half well or is only half awake, whatever she tries to do she throws herself 100% into that activity – whether it's being with her daughter Lydia, knitting, baking, crosswords, "manic" spring cleaning, singing, dancing, writing or making love. Other things Lorna enjoys are shopping and eating. Lorna makes a good shepherd's pie, cheese pie, and "truly irresistible" cheese scones – I might have the luck to taste one – if there are any left!

When Lorna has one of her many "down" days – either because of the illness or because of the side effects of her medication, she can only lie in bed until she has had enough rest and starts to feel better.

Since living with Lorna I've begun to appreciate the loneliness and isolation that goes with her Bipolar. She spends so much time on her own when she needs rest or extra sleep. I'd find that hard to cope with - I have at least 4 separate circles of friends, and I also use the mental health social group run by West Leicestershire Mind – so I never want for company. I feel really sorry for Lorna because sometimes the only person she sees for days on end - is me! How depressing! She could do with some regular female company. Also, Lorna plans to go to an event or go shopping – but on the day she's "not feeling very well" and doesn't go – so you see she really is very isolated. Lorna often makes plans to do so and so, or go here and there tomorrow but when tomorrow comes she might be disabled from doing whatever by her illness. So the planned tomorrow may actually be up to three weeks away.

When Lorna is down, I am quite tired with all of the household chores to do. When Lorna is on a high, she's hyperactive and full of energy – I can't keep up with her – she tires me out! I'm 17 years older than her, have type 2 diabetes, a slipped disc, depression and anxiety syndrome and post-traumatic stress disorder.

When on a "high" Lorna can spend 3, 4, 5, and even 12 or 17 hours at a stretch on whatever task she feels is absolutely vital at the time – sometimes it's crosswords, or knitting, or competitions on the internet, or writing, or bible study, or "chain watching" episodes of Prisoner Cell Block H or Dallas on DVD all night till 6 or 7am. Help!

When on a "high" Lorna's thoughts can run away with her and she talks too much and too fast – for instance on our honeymoon she was making plans for our first wedding anniversary! Also when on a high Lorna can indulge in manic spending either over the phone, on the internet or in person. She would spend all her money at once on shopping and not worry about paying bills or saving if I weren't there to remind her. She does of course have an occasional lapse – another 2 handbags, another 3 pairs of shoes, another 4 dresses, another 5 tops – but she can't help herself so shouldn't be judged (I used to be the same on buying DVDs – I'm a film buff and must have 800, it's one of my hobbies – although one of |Lorna's C.P.N.s described me as a hoarder – I'm not, I'm a collector!).

Lorna is also a very loving and passionate partner. I fell in love with her on our first date in 2002 (she actually did the asking) during which we had a drink or four, a Chinese takeaway by candlelight (it went cold because she insisted we use chopsticks), a cuddle or twenty, and even waltzed to the theme tune of Gone With The Wind on panpipes. I've always found her an extremely attractive woman, who has a great sense of fun. We split up after 3 months but started seeing each other again in 2009, I couldn't believe that for whatever reason she finally fell for me too – for once in my life I actually had some good luck for a change. Even if we are watching television we usually hold hands – until one of us gets cramp!

Of course, Lorna can be irritating at times – I'm supposed to have exclusive rights to the television at certain times – (it's in our verbal prenup agreement) – especially the four day Cheltenham horse racing festival in March – but during the running of the Champion Hurdle (they were actually halfway round) I got interrupted and asked "what sort of films do you like", "why" I asked – "because I'm on to Love Film about joining" – "war films and westerns" I replied - "name one" she asked – "How The West Was Won" I replied, "and I'm supposed to be watching the Cheltenham Festival!" – "sorry," she said – but I only saw the start and finish of a very important race.

As Lorna has already mentioned, she has a very poor memory, which she puts down to the E.C.T. treatment she had. She often forgets when she's booked appointments with the hairdresser, G.P., psychiatrist, dentist etc. etc.. She also forgets where she has put things – credit cards, keys, books, letters, mobile phone, pants, socks, tablets – we have spent up to four hours at a time looking for mislaid items – not one of my favourite pastimes! When we booked the appointment with the Registrar to arrange our wedding we had to provide details about one another – to catch out people arranging bogus marriages, Lorna was asked where I lived – she got that right, then she was asked what number – Lorna replied "11" the Registrar replied, "try 12". Lorna can also be forgetful and sometimes leaves the taps running, I've noticed her mum and daughter sometimes do the same – so taps must run in the family – noses run in mine (sorry).

Sometimes Lorna indulges in manic: talking, spending, or in enjoying one of her hobbies. So sometimes she interrupts what I'm doing or planning to do, so sometimes I get put out and have a chunter – "looks like I'm peeling the spuds again, preparing, cooking and serving the meal again, and doing the washing up again and again and again!" When we got married Lorna acquired a new dishwasher – me! Sometimes I need a break, and when out shopping pop to the pub for a couple beers, read the paper and do the crossword - yes I like crosswords too! When I wasn't coping mentally in the early part of our marriage I got referred to Good Thinking (mental health therapists who come to the G.P.s surgery to see you) and was, in turn, referred to Rethink who fixed us up with a Respite Carer to help me be giving me a break, and to help improve Lorna's confidence, skills, getting out and about and also Lorna gets to talk to another woman. Lorna's mood is always improved when she's been out to see the Respite Carer – usually at our local radio station's café – where Lorna attends a "knit and natter" group. Also, I was able to attend a Carers course run by Rethink – where I learnt more about mental illness, coping strategies, how to find help – support, financial, and information. While there I met other carers and we often exchanged notes – sometimes I went away thinking perhaps I don't have it too bad with Lorna – although with all the other carers caring for a spouse –the spouse had changed by becoming mentally ill after years of happy married life – I was the only one who had voluntarily married someone knowing that they were mentally ill. Like I said in my speech at our wedding "most people know Lorna and I met at a mental health social drop in – and we are both crazy – but only about each other!"

Poor Lorna has been experiencing severe panic attacks for a while now – sometimes at the mental health social group, or in busy shopping centres. Also once I nagged Lorna to go to see her doctor about a physical health problem – she refused to go – and only told me four days later that she was scared of walking out on her own – her doctors is only 400 yards from where we live – so I had to go with her. Personally, I believe she is suffering from agoraphobia. Lorna also has phobias about thunder and lightning (she has actually screamed on two occasions when there was a loud crash of thunder and a large flash of lightning), and also about strong winds – we were 30 yards from going inside a building when the wind suddenly got stronger and Lorna made moaning sounds and walked backwards the whole way – I think it's the wind blowing into her face that Lorna hates. She often just needs a reassuring hug to feel "safe and secure" – although if this leads to kissing it can take some time. Lorna says I'm a great kisser – it must be because I love her so much, because I've had very little practice at kissing.

Lorna also has a problem with her weight – she can usually stick to a healthy diet until after dinner time, but then often starts having snacks – she's never full. I don't know if this extra eating is caused by her illness, or it could be comfort eating, or it could be an increased appetite caused by her medication. It's a pity because Lorna tries really hard up to dinner and she can't be blamed for feeling hungry as a side effect of her illness or medication.

Sometimes I find myself living with someone who is detached, unaffectionate, difficult to speak to – I don't know how Lorna feels or what she thinks when she's like this – it can last for hours and sometimes days. Sometimes she can be quite snappy (like her first book "Snappy but Happy"). When she's like this I soldier on and remind myself that I love her, and that this is Lorna's illness – not Lorna herself; although understandably it often makes me snappy and grumpy too.

You can do a lot of things with Lorna – but the one thing you can never do is to stop her from doing something she's decided to do (even if it's not ultimately good for her) – it would be like trying to stop a runaway steamroller coming downhill toward you with your bare hands.

When Lorna's feeling well, confident or maybe when she's a little manic she can have a go at some activities that most other people would find pretty daunting – Lorna has now written and had published two books (this one and Snappy But Happy) – just writing and typing them is an effort, but you would be surprised how much goes on behind the scenes in getting them published – that's a major strength-sapping task on it's own. Also, Lorna found the courage to try the X Factor – she performed "my heart will go on" from Titanic, wearing an Abba costume. The costume was a good investment and certainly got her noticed, her singing was fine too – she passed two auditions and was filmed for her third audition but unfortunately didn't get through to the televised show.

Lorna's illness is a limiting and unrelenting illness – but although Lorna is often down, she is never down and out – she finds the strength and courage to keep coming back to battle "this monster of an illness" (her own description of Bipolar), and instead of anyone labelling her as "another one of them on benefits," they should give her a medal for never being totally defeated by Bipolar. It makes me proud to be the husband of such a beautiful, loving, strong and resilient woman.

As I said at the beginning Lorna is an amazing human being, and I love her to distraction.

PART TWO

CHAPTER 14

LORNA'S LATEST POEMS

GOING POTTY

The moment when young did
The moment I was a kid
I used to play mum against dad
I know as a youngster I wasn't that bad
Potty training was such a bore
I used to wee all over the floor
Now I'm older I do it in the loo
Sometimes I don't make it when I need a poo!

THE BEACH

I like to stroll along the beach
With soft silky sand beneath my feet
This is a rare treat
With the tropical sun shining in my face
The perfect paradise place
The waves of the sea crash to and fro
The boats in the harbour have far to go
Some pleasure some pain
This is what I have to gain
Little crabs scurry everywhere
One crawled in my underwear!

POOR OLD TOM

I know a cat called
Tom I don't where he's from
He often roams the street at night
Beware when there's a mouse in sight
Poor old Tom lost his dinner
He crossed the road and got hit by a car
That'll teach him to roam too far
He thought he had nine lives
When of course he only had one
Now poor Tom is gone.

FREE AS A BIRD

As I watch the sun and the sea from the skies above, I feel free as a bird,
Roaming to and fro across the sun's reflected glow,
I fly across the breadth of the watery deep,
Searching for something tasty to eat.

Rising high in the sky, I fly, with my wings taking me to the parallel of the universe,
I soar like an eagle about to pounce on its prey.
My talons, razor like and sharp, pierce deep into the bark.
The trees reflect my shadow, that's waiting to pounce upon any tasty morsel that passes me by,
I can fly; I'm free as a bird.

THE BALANCE OF NATURE

I love nature this true,
I often like to visit the zoo.
There are lions, tigers, monkeys and camels,
These are all perfect mammals,
I like to see them in their habitats.
You'll find my favourite are the Meerkats.

Lions and tigers all penned up in their cages,
Thinking we haven't been out in ages.
I often like to watch them pacing to and fro,
Waiting for their next unexpected victim to show.

In the wild, if an antelope should stray,
The pride would say, let us prey.
I often love to see monkeys swinging from trees, eating bananas and doing as they please.

Wild and free, like animals should be,
One day all animals will be set loose,
They won't be caged; they'll be a truce,
To roam free as God intended,
Animals and man will be befriended.

VITAL FOR LIFE

Water we need to stay alive,
Without it we would simply die,
It sustains us in our hour of need,
This is an excellent commodity indeed.

A precious gift we indeed do have,
Although water is very scarce,
Some have to dig for water in wells,
Where some people take water for granted like they often do,
We should learn to live and share, with this product that is so rare.

THE BREEZE

With the breeze and the falling leaves, I look up and feel really at ease,
They are crinkly and crunchy at my feet,
I sit beneath a tree in the autumn sun, I feel the heat.

The sound of many birds fills the woods,
When I close my eyes I feel a gentle breeze upon the nape of my neck,
The golden sun is glowing,
It enlightens my heart.

The breeze from the trees sends a shiver down my spine,
It is absolutely divine.

GETTING UP IN THE MORNING

I feel so warm; I don't want to move,
Wrapped up so snugly in my bed,
I often feel like a sleepy head.

I slowly open my eyes and to my surprise,
The alarm went off an hour past,
It's time to get up, I gasp.

Sometimes I don't get up at all,
I often need a wake up call,
This is often how I feel,
Getting up in the morning is so unreal.

It's like torture to my brain,
Getting up in the morning drives me insane.

Pete my hubby brings me breakfast in bed,
Along with my insulin and mental health med,
Sometimes he provides me with a cuppa,
Sometimes I don't get up till supper.

The feelings I have aren't really me,
Sometimes I don't feel in control you see,
I often experience disturbing thoughts,
Of suicide I'm out of sorts.

However to me prayer is a must,
I know it's in God I put my trust,
I ask for strength, especially when I'm low.

The pills I take make me go,
There are side effects from the pills,
These are part of my Bipolar ills.

WATER- A REFRESHING TONIC

Water we need to keep us strong,
There are many without and that is wrong,
Without enough to sustain use we would simply die,
Without water you couldn't even cry,

Water is a marvellous gift from God from up above,
We should learn to share this commodity with love,
Many of us take for granted the little that we have,
Many haven't got any and that to me is bad.

So the moral of the poem is to make folk understand,
That water is so precious and scarce in other lands.

So don't waste water, conserve what you can,
Cos one day you'll never know we might be under ban,
This rare commodity is a blessing there's no doubt,
So don't waste water cos we can't do without.

AM I GOING MAD?

The thoughts within my brain are driving me insane,
The thoughts inside my head have almost gone dead,
My brain feels empty like a sieve,
This is often how I live.

A chemical imbalance makes me think wrong thoughts,
I misbehave, I'm out of sorts,
I was guilty of no crime, just ill and sectioned for a time,
I was diagnosed with Postnatal depression
However this wasn't true,
The quacks got it all wrong like they sometimes do.

I was misdiagnosed there's no doubt,
I have Bipolar which affects the mind,
It's a part of me that I have declined.

I'm up one minute and down the next,
My mood swings vary and I get perplexed,
I tell you one thing that keeps me sane,
That's doing crosswords which helps my brain.

CHAPTER 15

PETE'S POEMS

SERENE SUICIDE (1991)

No more stress, no more strain,
No more sorrow, no more pain,
No more longing, unfilled desire,
No more failure, as I expire.

No more anger, no more fear,
No old age, dying year by year,
No fearful future, no tortured past,
Suicide's sweet release, serene at last.

WE WILL REMEMBER THEM (1995)

What's this V.E. Day, V.J. Day
Business really all about,
It's just to say we won the war,
That's without a doubt.

It's what happened to this world of ours,
In the Second World War,
How can people think it
Shouldn't be remembered any more?

Hitler's SS Nazi legions covered most of our continent,
Mussolini's fascists to Albania and Abyssinia went,
Hirohito's fanatics oppressed most of the Far East,
Evil that was man made the nature of the beast.

Britain's share of the sacrifice, to put the world to right,
Sixty-two thousand civilians killed, by bombing in the night,
The gallant merchant seamen, lost thirty-five thousand men,
And three hundred thousand fighting men never breathed again.

Fifty-four million was the estimated world death toll,
Seventeen million in uniform heard the deathly knoll,
Non combatant – civilian dead – in millions twenty seven,
Six million Poles, ten million Chinese, fourteen million Russian.

Six million Jews, unknown numbers of European Gipsy,
All these non combatants murdered – cleansed ethically,
However unsatisfactory whatever took its place
The victory of the Allies saved the human race.

V.E. Day, V.J. Day are still something to commemorate,
For all the enslaved millions they helped to liberate,
They put an end to evil, wholesale, global genocide
Without these victories how many more millions would have died?

CONSUMER (2000)

Instead of salmon – I bought tuna
- to be a bit more trendy,

The tin's label proudly said
-that it was dolphin friendly,

I thought you've done your bit
-But I wish I'd been greener sooner

Then later realised
- I hadn't been very friendly to the tuna.

AGORAPHOBIC (2001)

Have you ever walked a lonely street and felt all alone?
Like Gary Cooper in High Noon,
Have you ever felt isolated in a town full of people?
Like the last human being in The Invasion Of The Body Snatchers.

Have you ever felt the whole world shrink and close in only on you?
That everyone is staring at you,
And knows your complete history,
Is it the others who are different or is it me, is it me?

It is not the fear of public places,
It is the fear of the fear that races –
The pulse, causing sweating, shortness of breath,
Sometimes vomiting, I'm scared to death.

I always make an effort, I try to defy,
But sometimes it beats me, I fail, I cry,
To others, it may appear that it's all unreal,
They don't live in my head, this is how I feel.

SORRY I'M A BENEFIT CLAIMANT (2001)

I'm sorry that I've failed to fulfil
Society's hopes for me because I fell ill.

I'm agoraphobic, clinically depressed, so give me my due,
At times suicidal, I tried six times, and failed at that too.

Society looks for me to take all the blame
After seven years I've started to feel less shame.

Not being fit for work is my unforgivable sin
They say nothing of the 22 years I paid in.

Sometimes vile memories pierce my mind in the day
Sometimes in nightmares I relive them again on replay.

Forced to revive and relive the endless heartaches
Of a thousand past painful, tearful mistakes.

I now seem to live in a no tolerance zone
No wonder I retreat further into a world of my own.

I've been raped and molested; this world's not been kind,
And worse I've been denied my potential of heart and mind.

I no longer feel I have anything more to atone
I just wish other people would leave me alone.

So all you ignorant judgemental people out there
Give me a break to endure my own private despair.

THE BELLS (2002)

It's singing, pinging, ringing,
Should I answer it?
Is it a friend or a fiend?
Is it good news,
Or telesales interviews?

All I say is a polite "hello"
For this offence
My ears are bombarded
With verbal d
From Kelly -It's her career
To trespass on my ear.

She's pleased to inform me
"This is not a sales call" (Not at all)
"You've been selected by our computer
For five hundred pounds off
Our double glazing Isn't that amazing!"

And "would you like a porch
Or perhaps a patio?
Does your guttering fascia
Need repainting?"

Gasp
Kelly's nearly fainting
She hasn't paused for breath.

But I'm in at the death
As into the Phone
I intone
The magic words
To make her disappear.

"THIS IS A COUNCIL HOUSE."

She puts her phone down
Quiet as a mouse.
I hang up.

Again,
It's singing, pinging, ringing.
Should I answer it?

Is it a friend or a fiend?
Is it good news?
Or more telesales interviews!

NIGHT (2003)

Sunshine into twilight
Warmth into chill
Stark shapes into shadows
Motion into still.

Innocence into menace
Gentle breezes into howling horrors
Creaky floorboards into intruders
Trees into clutching terrors.

Pussies into growling panthers
Parties into revels
Teddies into grizzlies
Dolls into devils

Confidence into concern
Order into mess
Space into claustrophobia
Solitude into loneliness

Reality into make believe

Joy into sorrow

Day dreams into nightmares

Today into tomorrow.

CHRISTMAS TRUCE 1914 (2004)

The men rose up – the rank and file

Leaving trenches, stretching mile on mile,

In No Man's land – peace for a day

By "Private" arrangement – the generals had no say.

There was little grass for the pitch

Craters of mud stretched to either ditch

Harry passed the ball to Jack

Karl intercepted and passed back –

To Fritz. The whistle signalled play to stop

It usually meant over the top.

Harry shared whisky and schnapps with Karl,

Jack gave Fritz Woodbines, he got a cigar,

Harry wished Karl " Merry Christmas mate"

"Ja kamarade" Karl replied, presenting chocolate.

On Boxing Day the shelling started at dawn,

Christians awake salute the happy morn.

The Germans launched their mass attack

Against yesterday's Pals, Harry and Jack.

Harry took careful aim, and fired,

For Karl a silent night - as he expired.

That evening Harry shed a secret tear

For Christmas comes but once a year.

TREE FELLA (2007)

I've stood here since before
Bosworth Field,
My brothers were felled
To make ships for Nelson.

You look at me
And see just a tree
Possibly think me dead wood.

But I've been alive
Ten times longer than
Man's three score
Years and ten.

I have an important job
To maintain nature's balance
I recycle air, my leaves
Create chlorophyll from sunlight.

My roots mine the earth
To siphon unseen, untapped water,
My arms stretch out wide
To welcome birds
But no woodpeckers please.

You are born, grow, live and die
Too fast to notice me
Because I grow more slowly.

Yet I live, and have been
Greener a lot longer than you have
I'm unnoticed because you can't
See the tree for the woods.

I CANNOT BLEED (2007)

The red leaf is dying
It's two eyes have been crying.

The red leaf's edges have curled
But it is not a life raft.

The red leaf overturned has a long tail
But it is not a mouse.

The red leaf rustled in the wind
But has never heard music.

The red leaf has veins
But cannot bleed.

(UNSEEN) (2007)

How can you be off on the sick?
No wheelchair, not even a walking stick,
Display these badges and we'll sympathise
Without – for not working we'll despise.

You see, we haven't got the facility
To comprehend your disability
Perhaps you could display on card
How you have it so really hard.

The days of depression – no energy
The nights without sleep, we cannot see
The suicide attempts, when it's really bad,
Loss of judgement, is this real, or am I mad?

And what's the reason you're this way
Oh sorry, you were raped you say.
Right, next time we see someone like you

When you say you're ill – we'll take it as true.

QUESTIONS TO A DEAD LEAF IN THE WATER (2007)

Do you feel wet?
Can you feel the heat?
Do you miss not having feet?

Do you go out a lot?
Do you miss your mother the tree?
What do you think about global warming?

Do you support Notts. Forest?
Should I recycle you to help
Other plants live?

Where do you see yourself
In five years time?

I WOULD WORRY (2007)

When I used to go
To Social occasions
A meal, a pint, a party
I would worry.

I would worry
Will I arrive on time?
Will my bus, taxi, lift turn up?
Will I get home OK?

I would worry
Will I be the worst one there?
Will I find a seat
With an escape route?
If I'm blocked in
I'll be anxious throughout.

I would worry
What if the loo is occupied?
And I have to use a urinal –
And someone else comes in?
If so I can't always go.

Others just turned up
Without their negative thoughts,
I would feign diplomatic diarrhoea So as not to undergo
The private self torture Of my own anxieties.

UNNATURAL (2007)

Millions of years ago
The earth's heartbeat
Pulsating magma through its mantle
Coating the land with granite.

Dense woodland carpeted virgin soil
Eons before man first stood upright
To claim the land as his alone.

River, stream, lake, pool
Sustained life
Later diverted to fill canals
And brew Burton's beer.

Timber, clay, granite slate
Plundered to build
Man's unnatural habit- housing
Warriors, farmers, merchants, barons.

And nuns at Gracedieu,
Monks at Ulverscroft.
Coal was mined to heat homes,
Power industry, steam engines, ships.

Trees grew naturally for
Millions of years
Before man arrived to put
A spanner in natures works.

Will future generations think
Our past sins expunged
By our planting a few trees
To redress the balance?

Or will they judge us
As vandals and thieves?

SECRET SOLITUDE (2007)

At Cheltenham races
Lost in the crowd
I experienced a panic attack.

Seeking a refuge
I found a bench
(away from the hurly burly)
With views of Cleeve Hill –
An ocean of green,
Dotted with stepping stones
Of Cotswold cottages.

A lifeboat In a sea
Of ten thousand souls –
All swimming spermlike
To be the first
To fulfil each quest –
A pint, a punt, a pee.

Bookies shouting the odds –
Were drowned out
By it's compelling silence.
Fresh air, mixed with whiffs
Of new mown grass –
And frying onions.

It felt satisfying
And comforting –
Like a warming soup
On a winter's night.

In my secret solitude –
Each blade of grass
Whispered –
This is your spiritual home.

LORNA MURBY

In my secret solitude –
Each blade of grass
Whispered
Here is a safe haven
From the panic of life.

POSTCARDS FROM EVEREST (2002)

Launch Failure *Come on! Come on!*
No response.
In the prison of my armchair,
My leg muscles stiffen, in defiance
of my will. I'm unable to stand.
I'm locked in
by my fear of going out.

Lift Off

Come on! Come on!
Hallelujah
We have lift off!
I launch myself
From my chair,
It's only taken forty
Minutes to suppress my
fear today.
Most days I don't
Make it out at all.

Checking

Still inside the house
checking everything's off
and doors and windows
are locked.
Look outside to check
if there's anyone about
who I usually avoid.
Good, the coast is clear.
Unlock front door, go out,
lock the door.
Check three times that
I've locked it.
Check I've got the key.

Weather check

Pity it's not raining.
I like the rain.
People don't bother with
Me when it's raining,
so I feel less anxious
when it's wet.

Cunning Plan

Good, planned to leave home
before 9a.m. It's the holidays,
should be no kids about, early
doors. No one in sight. Arrive
safely at the top of the street.
Gasp. Sigh.

Busy Bodies

Turn into main road, lots
of busy people walking to work
and the shops.
Hurrying, Scurrying,
Hustling, Bustling.

Distraction

Why am I going dizzy.
Come on, try to breathe deeply,
slowly to lessen the symptoms.
To take my mind of my fear,
I silently whistle a tune
"Scipio" from Trooping
The Colour.

Out of Step

Oh dear, I'm marching
in step to the music again.
It looks silly, but it transports
me from A to B.
People are staring at me,(aren't they?)

Stoppage

Tittering coming from behind me.
Someone's humming The British
Grenadiers very loudly. I slow down,
stop, pretend to check my bag.
Get overtaken by a mother and
three children – who all managed
to get up before nine.

Wrong Angles

The pavements moving up and down,
The road's at an angle of thirty degrees,
oh no it's blurred vision again1
Are my eyes getting enough oxygen?
No my fear has released adrenalin,
and it is in control of my body, not me,
ordering my blood to the wrong places.

Reality Check

I feel dizzy, nauseous,
have chest pains, and
my vision is still distorted.
Every step I take, I look down
as I slowly plant my foot onto
the pavement. The pavement is
level really – it's just my eyes
playing tricks on me.

Control

Right the agoraphobia is
really bad today – so just concentrate on walking
And not falling over. I breathe slowly and deeply
to reduce the effects of the symptoms – and
to regain control of my own mind and body.

Decision Time

Decide whether to continue
into the heart of the town –
full of people, to get stares,
glances and commentary from
the crowds, and to experience
heightened agoraphobia,
OR
attempt the short cut over
the foot bridge? Less time out
over the bridge, less anxiety for
me, but it's the bridge where
an innocent man was beaten up
by five thugs a few weeks ago
-so will I be safe?

The Rubicon

Take a deep breath, send
some oxygen to my remaining
brain cells so I can decide.
Cross at the Green Man
that's OK for either option.

Safety Check

Glance through the steps of
the bridge – has fate decreed
it's my day to be beaten up?
Is anyone laying in wait for me?
No, right - left turn to the bridge.

Base Camp

Arrive at the foot of the bridge.
Too scared to climb over it.
Come on – breathe – come on
it's not Mount Everest, oh yes it is
to me!

Conquest

Come on just do it. For once
just do it – without thinking
about it. Deep breath, come on
start to climb the steps. Hooray
made it to the top safely! In reality
it's not the highest place on Earth -
But in my distorted view of life it is.

Negativity

OK I conquered my fear today,
tomorrow I probably won't even
be able to get out of the chair, even
if I do will I want to suffer the
hardship of climbing Everest again?
It's easier to stay in. Why do I
Have to undergo this torture all the time?

WHO AM I? (2008)

I am not Linford Christie
- I haven't brought my
Snooker cue with me.

I am not Lang Lang
- But I can play chopsticks.

I am not
The Duke of Westminster
- I've left my four days of
Washing up at home.

I am not Cassanova
- But I've had my moments

I am not
Einstein
- But I can solve
A crossword.

Yet I
Cannot solve the riddle
of myself.

POWERLESS (2008)

Poor Coalville – once vital, steam whistles called
- miners to graft
- down the shaft

Now it's shrivelled,
as good as dead,
a ghost town, the Pits.

Black seams abandoned - scrapped,
potential energy – untapped,
collieries, communities, people – redundant
    - no more coal, creating electricity,
no more power.

Now all that's left to mark
our mining heritage
- Snibston Discovery Park
- but how to visit?

On the internet it is said
    - if travelling by rail
"passengers alight at Loughborough
or Leicester instead"
for Coalville, your destination
hasn't even got a station.

What ingratitude!
Did Dr Beeching not know
that we built the second railway
in the world at Coalville!

At Snibston
    - the winding wheel above the town
stigmatic of our industrial decline
not a museum – a shrine
beneath which is buried
our town's soul
a not long dead monarch
King Coal.

LOST AT YPRES (2012)

He is lost somewhere, generations ago,
Forgotten in the fog of the past.
Perhaps he went "over the top"
His only protection – a helmet of steel.

Men fell all around him
- like confetti scattered at a wedding
- staining the muddy field
poppy red with blood.

Other men torn by machine gun fire
were stuck on the "old barbed wire"
- like obscene ornaments on a Christmas tree,
I wonder how did he expire?
Was he killed by bullet, bayonet or gas
or shell? Or was he wounded only to
slip and slide and drown in the muddy morass?
At Passchendaele.

For freedom his young life he gave
he is one of the fifty-five thousand
with his name chiselled on the Menin Gate
who have no known grave.

Buried anonymously beneath the sod,
his headstone reading :
"A British Soldier of The Great War
Known unto God."

REMEMBER HIM

(Written after a visit to the Menin Gate, Ypres
and Tyne Cot Military Cemetery, Passchendaele.)

THE ICEBERG (2011)

People only see the tenth of me,
that I let them see,
the rest of me, like an iceberg
is unseen,
submerged in the ice cold sea
of my mind.

My life defining moment
came when I was eight
a "Titanic" experience,
my future snatched away
from me by a chance
encounter with a stranger.

I was frozen with fear
emotionally dead,
as cold as a corpse
in a mortuary,
my own private self
hidden from view for fifty years.

A secret hidden person,
wondering why I had no ambition,
- unable to ask a woman out
let alone to say "I love you"
- unable to speak about myself
- unable to ask for help.

Happiest when left alone
or hidden by others in a crowd, I hated standing out
drawing attention to myself.
All I wanted was to remain hidden.

Recently through counselling
forty odd years of delayed

shock was unleashed
- I threw up three times,
- cried for hours, for months
at a time.

The images stayed with me
awake, and in nightmares
for some time,
for the first time I was able
to face up to what had been
imposed on me by a stranger
physically, mentally, emotionally.

Now enjoying the warmth
of humanity, a warmth
that has made me melt
like a snowman in summertime
- now no longer on my own
trapped in a vice of ice
- but freed to live a life
joining humanity
joining the sea.

JUST FOR A DAY (2013)

I'd make the mentally ill well
And see the hungry fed
I'd see the homeless sleep in a bed.

I'd see disabled people walk I
'd see the silent talk
But make the politicians mute.

I'd reward the victims of crime
By doubling the sentences time
And by closing the open prisons.

I'd cancel all debt
All mobiles to silent set
I'd abolish the "F" word yet.

I'd let the bullied prevail
Make the bullies know fear
Maybe make them shed a tear.

I'd take the PG chimps to see
A political party
To see if can tell any difference.

We'd leave the EU
It's long overdue
I'd make Eurostar
End at Waterloo
(like Napoleon).

I'd abolish all nightmares
But make dreams come true
If just for a day you became me
And I became you.

THE SACRIFICED VICTIM (2013)

From the solitary confinement of my brain,
I've tried to tell others, but can't explain
About my private prison of pain
My illnesses – post traumatic stress disorder
Anxiety and depression syndrome.

Did I choose to be this way?
No! This was imposed on me
When I was raped at eight
Frightened out of my wits
By his threat to murder me
If I told
I believed him and never did.

The criminal has evaded punishment
I the innocent have had to serve
This life sentence of sorrow
Yesterday, today and tomorrow.

I've really tried my best
But there's no escape for me
Not even in rest
Horrific nightmares burgle my sleep
Robbing me of peace.

The victim – now I'm to be put on trial
For being ill, new forms to fill
How can I communicate all this
When they don't ask
The questions relevant to me
To disprove my fitness.

So I won't get the boxes ticked
So eventually I'll be picked
To be considered for work
I've been tricked.

I thought I was safe, saved
But I'm to be sacrificed
Butchered on the altar of
Welfare reform, enslaved
Society's scapegoat to take the blame
For someone else's sin. Shame!

Not guilty. But punished.
Justice perverted by a pervert.
No appeal. No pardon.
No apology.
Is it me who's sick
Or is it Society?

So push me further than I can go
So I get worse and have to go
One final throw of life's dice
The "S" word
The ultimate sacrifice.

ODE TO IDS (2013)

From IB and DLA
Through ESA to JSA
I may get the PIP.

No help from NHS or DSS
Now DWP and JCP
More like Hitler's SS.

Oh what a mess
I'm in the S!

Thank you IDS
You gave ATOS
A lot of dosh
I'm at a loss.

Oh what a mess
I'm in the S!

(For the unaffected)
IDS = Ian Duncan Smith (Minister for Works and Pensions)
IB = Incapacity Benefit
DLA = Disability Living Allowance
ESA = Earnings Support Allowance (replacing IB)
PIP = Personal Independence Payment (replacing DLA)
NHS = National Health Service
DSS = Department of Social Security
DWP = Department of Work and Pensions JCP = Job Centre Plus
ATOS = Private Foreign Company paid to assess individual's Limited Capability for Work Questionnaire.

IT'S RAINING AGAIN! (2013)

It's almost unthinkable
Only 1% of water is drinkable.

Without water the Earth would be a desert of death
   - No water, no plants, no animals, no breath.

We take our water supply for granted
Imagine if we were suddenly transplanted

- To Africa and Asia, where mother and daughter
Trek miles to fetch and carry water.

So now give thanks, that we know the reason
For our yearlong British rainy season!

IMPRESSIONS (2013)

Inviting, warm azure sea
Warm virgin sands beneath my feet,
My footmarks fill with water
As the tide comes in
Then all trace of me disappears
As at the ebb flow of life.

POETIC LICENCE (2007)

Here's a little ditty
All regular and pretty
De Dumb, De Dumb, De Dumb,
De Dumb, De Dumb, De Dumb.

I'm no slave to ironic perimeter,
I won't be confined to a set metre
Which is made up of feet anyway
So shouldn't that be in yards?

Does a poem have to rhyme?
Well perhaps in shards
But not all the time.

How many lines to a verse?
Or how many sillybells
The jokes on you
I don't use haiku.

I just enjoy writing verse.
However strange and perverse
Not proper poetry

So judge me on my words I pray
I'm free from form
At least for today.

FROM WELFARE TO WORKHOUSE (2013 NOT 1813)

My debts and credit situation,

As with many others in our nation

- Are slowly strangling me

- Like a noose around my throat

- That's so tight I cannot undo the knot.

We only need to be cut a little slack

- Then hopefully we might get into the black

- But we're so deeply in the red

I'm so worried, everyday I wish I was dead.

Day to day, week to week, swallow any pride

- A constant struggle to decide

Which direct debit to cancel next

- And which bill we dare leave unpaid

- And what things to go without I'm afraid.

We look forward to those days we get paid

- Go "Wow" and think we've got it made

- Then pay off some arrears

- But it always ends in tears

- When we find we have so little left.

It was the 2013 "bedroom" tax that hit us hard

- We're seventy pounds a month worse off

(After ten months that's £700)

We'll soon find all future credit barred

So no hope of yet another credit card.

So deeper and deeper we'll sink in debt

- And we haven't had the electricity and gas increases yet.

No hope, no joy, no future

But soon we'll be eligible to sign up

To a new bank – the food bank.

In 1930, my father who was ten years old,
Queued at the soup kitchen at the end of the road,
To collect soup for himself and widowed mother,
His little sister and little brother.

This government took money from those in need
- To cut millionaires taxes – we're paying for their greed,
- This government instead of looking after it's own – us
Prefers to give aid to India so they can send a rocket to Mars
Or aid to Africa so Presidents can buy jets or flash new cars
While sometimes I struggle to pay for a ride on the bus.

Electricity, gas, and water now privately owned
By foreign companies
Whose only object to make more profits can't be condoned
So again we seem back in the nineteen thirties
Do we need to elect a government to nationalise "Public" utilities?

The Welfare State and what a state it's in
The poor struggle to fill a plate
We've returned to the "Hard Times" of Dickens
- For I've had to sell items at a Pawnbrokers
- One of this government's business growth successes
Along with charity shops and Poundland.

So at the next election
I won't forget who put us in this plight
-This government and a bunch of bankers
- I'm not sure I've spelt that right.

I LOVE YOU LORNA XXXX (2010)

When we are together
- It is bliss.
Apart I miss
- The taste of your kiss
The touch of your skin.

I love you Lorna
XXXX

You are beautiful
I love your face, your hair
Your lips, your bust
The pretty mole on your tum
Your silky legs, and your bum.

I love you Lorna
XXXX

Love is not governed
By reason, or by time
Love's like art, music or rhyme
- It's clouded in mystery
- Two hearts as one – symmetry.

I love you Lorna
XXXX

If we were granted
One day only
- To join as one
In making love
- Then to make
That day last forever
- I'd stop the earth
From turning.

I love you Lorna
XXXX

PART THREE

CHAPTER 16

PETE'S SHORT STORIES

DEAD LUCKY (2007)

There was no Sequence Dance at the church hall this Saturday. Mabel and Fred had just finished supper – homemade shepherds pie, with homegrown carrots from Fred's allotment.

"I've cleared the plates for you to wash up, and put out a clean pinny – the old one's in the wash" instructed Mabel as she entered the living room.

"Shush" pleaded Fred. "Number 10" – "yes," said Fred. "Number 5" – "yes". "Number 42" – "Yes" shouted Fred.

"Oh good," said Mabel. "The last three numbers on the National Lottery. I could buy a new Mac and handbag from the charity shop, or we could go mad next week and have a Hawaiian pineapple and ham takeaway Pizza."

Fred pictured the virgin white sand of the beach, the hot sun burning down, himself in Bermuda shorts shaded beneath the palms, gently rubbing suntan lotion onto a bronzed, long-legged busty blonde – wearing just a thong, sipping on something long and cool through pouted lips.

"......and don't forget tomorrow, when we go to me sisters, you can pick her some veg from the allotment – oh and I said you'd look at that gate of hers that's hanging off the hinges."

"Yes, dear" complied Fred.

"Oh Casualty's on – I don't want to miss the start. Since you've been messing about in here – you might as well make the cocoa – after washing up."

"Yes, dear."

Fred entered the kitchen, - closed the door, took the lottery ticket out of his cardigan pocket and kissed it. "Last three numbers be buggered, I've got the first three an all" he chuckled. Fred put on his clean pinny, the one with intertwined roses, and not wanting to spend too much too soon – he flicked through the Argos catalogue looking for a coffin!

CLOSE SHAVE (2007)

Surgeon: "Good morning, have you any questions about what we're actually going to do in the operation, or about any after effects?"

Male Patient: "The other surgeon I saw at Out-Patients covered most of it, but there was something I've been wondering about – how long will it be till I can pee with some degree of comfort?"

Surgeon: "That depends on how quickly things heal up – it'll feel a little tender for at least four to six weeks, I will of course try to damage the urethra as little as possible."

Patient: "Well I suppose that can't be helped – with what you're going to do. I should have had it done years ago, but it'll be a big relief for me when it's finally over."

Surgeon: "Yes you do seem to have left it a bit late. By the way you should be on the table for about six hours – and you'll be feeling a little groggy for some time afterwards."

Patient: "SIX hours – the other chap said less than two."

Surgeon: "Oh I'm sorry – I see in your notes it mentions that you feel nervous about the surgery, I suppose my colleague told you a little white lie to put you more at ease. Now if you could just take off your trousers and underpants, and pull your shirt up. Ignore what I'm doing – I'm just going to draw on you with a felt tip pen, where I'm going to make my incisions – you might feel a little tickle."

Patient: "Excuse me, I thought you'd be getting close, but why have you drawn a circle all around the base of my penis – I thought you'd be a good two or three inches away at least."

Surgeon: "I'm not sure you're ready for the operation yet – I think you're a little in denial – surely in counselling you must have come to terms with having it removed – I mean that's pretty fundamental in a gender reassignment."

Patient: "I know I'm only the patient – but don't you think a sex change is rather drastic – I only came in here because I have an enlarged prostrate!"

ONE GOOD TURN (2002)

It was John and Jane's lucky night, they matched five numbers and the bonus ball on the Saturday Lottery, winning £350,000. They were both in their early fifties, in jobs they only tolerated. Their first action was to take early retirement from their respective posts.

They were a quiet, easygoing, solid, respectable, happily married couple. Their long term pipe dream was to live in archetypical, clichéd English country cottage. After several months of careful and enjoyable searching, their dream was realised. The road ran across an ancient stone bridge over the stream, past the Norman church, village green, pub, post office and scores of immaculately kept "picture postcard" cottages. On a bend was a single storey, detached thatched Tudor timbered cottage, fronted by a small rose garden. Deducting the value of their own home, it would only cost them a net £60,000.

They had no care for the high life or jet set, and weren't going to spend, spend, spend. They had been unable to have children, and had no close relatives still alive to share their good fortune with. They decided to donate £20,000 to various charities, and gave an anonymous £10,000 to enable a local six year old girl to go to the states for life-saving medical treatment.

John and Jane sold their old home, moved into their dream cottage, and settled down to life in this peaceful idyll. Peaceful apart from the occasional juggernaut that threaded its way through the village's meandering narrow lanes. A bypass that was near completion would soon remove the only irritant in their otherwise perfect world.

The months passed happily by, and they found that they fitted in with most of the other villagers – many of whom had retired there, like themselves.

One morning John and Jane got up, breakfasted and found they had an E-mail waiting. It read:

"John, I must see you and Jane on Friday morning at the village church at ten o'clock. I know something about your past that neither of you would want to get into the newspapers. Don't be late! Jacob Malwhinnie.

John checked for an address to reply to, but the impotent machine only informed that the E-mail address read "unknown."

John and Jane racked their memories, thinking of minor misdemeanours either of them might have committed in the past. They couldn't bring anything to mind, and assumed someone had found out about their lottery win, and was attempting some absurd form of blackmail – but about what.

They checked the phonebook but surprise, surprise there was no one listed under Malwhinnie. They hadn't enough evidence to involve the police, and worried as to how they should proceed. John wanted to face the blackmailer alone, but Jane insisted on coming with him. Although Jane had implicit trust in John, it crossed her mind that he might have fathered a child by some "other women" and wanted it kept secret – especially from herself. After all Jane was 100% certain that she had no skeletons hidden in her past.

Friday morning arrived, and at 9.30 John tried to dissuade Jane from accompanying him on the secret rendezvous. Jane however was driven by her own curiosity, and refused to be sidestepped. They were both bewildered and frightened, despite John trying to act in an over the top macho manner.

They arrived at the church at 9.45 to discover no one in sight. They decided to walk around the church, in case their mysterious nemesis was lurking, unseen round the back. There was still no one in sight.

At one minute to ten, John stopped in his tracks and called Jane over to the gravestone he was looking at. The inscription on the stone read "Jacob Malwhinnie, 1890 – 1955 R.I.P.." John choked out loud "someone's idea of a practical joke, or the modern equivalent of a poison pen letter."

On the stroke of ten, John and Jane heard the shrill screech of brakes, followed by a loud bang – the sound of a heavy collision. A few seconds later they heard the boom of a deafening explosion. They turned around, and to their horror saw their cottage
half-demolished, and engulfed in an inferno of flame. The tanker driver had jumped clear into the safety of their rose garden.

After the fire brigade had extinguished the blaze, there was little of their now nightmare cottage left standing. At least they were both alive and unhurt and the cottage was insured. In their next-door neighbour's cottage, over gigantic medicinal brandies, John managed to change the subject. "Have you lived in the village for long?" he asked their human St Bernard.

The old gentleman replied, "I was born here – seventy five years ago."

John continued "Don't think I'm off my head for asking you this, but did you know a Jacob Malwhinnie who died in the fifties, at all?"

The old man creased his face in thought, and then replied "Yes of course I remember old Jake. His family moved away and lost touch with the village. Mind you, his granddaughter was in the local paper a few months back – her daughter had a life saving operation in America."

CHAPTER 17

LYDIA'S SHORT STORIES

Twins Forever!

~Chloe ~

I love the way he looks. His brown hair, so soft and silky. His eyes, blue as the sea. You probably think I'm writing about my boyfriend but you're wrong. I was describing my brother. He's not older, nor is he younger. He's my twin.

Chase always makes me laugh and he's always there for me. He's my best friend and always has my back. I know this and it gives me courage when I walk into the school grounds, but that won't keep me from being afraid for long.

As I look around, I see Kyle standing by the fence. As soon as he sees me, a smirk grows on his face and a wicked gleam appears in his eyes. I quickly lower my head as I walk past hastily. I know he's going to get me at break time. I just know it. Heading into school, I went to the school's library and got a book. I bury my head into it and try to focus on the story, but the words swirl around the page and my heart starts pounding. I know what's going to happen. Where's Chase right now? Oh wait...he's probably hanging around with his mates. I usually tell him everything. We've never ever kept secrets from each other, but I can't tell him about this. He probably won't believe me anyway, no one will.

I try to focus on the book again but I just can't. I then hear the door open and my mouth runs dry, my palms starting to sweat as I feel myself trembling. *Oh no! He followed me here! What should I do?! I'm trapped!* Panicked, I try to hide behind the book I'm holding, in desperation, but to no avail, as he sees me anyway. He snatches the book out of my hand and tosses it on the floor. I'm then violently shoved, causing me to topple backwards in my chair, hitting my head on the floor. "Stop it! P-please! J-just leave me alone!" I whimper.

He snorts loudly, laughing at me, "What a cry baby! What? You hoping your mummy is going to come and wipe your little eyes? Pathetic!" This is not the end. It's only the beginning of what's to come.

~Chase~

Okay! So I'm just casually hanging out with my mates, Joe and Carlos. I should be laughing at their jokes and messing around with them like a fool. Like I always usually do. But I can't! I'm worried about Chloe. She's hiding something from me. I can feel it. I don't know what it is, but I have such a bad feeling about it. She also keeps disappearing when we get home. Something really isn't right here, and I know it!

Every day when we walk to the school ground, I see the fear grow rapidly in her eyes as arrive. Her head lowers to the ground as she refuses to look at anything. Sometimes I swear I can almost see her trembling. The same thoughts constantly pass through my mind, over and over again. *What's bothering her? What's she so afraid of? What's going on? And why won't she tell me?* I have to get to the bottom of this. When we get home, I'm going to talk to her about it. At school, it would be too much in the open.

As I look around the grounds, I notice it's pretty empty and that's when I realise the bell must have gone already. Quickly, I rush inside and head to the classroom. I'm most likely going to get told off by Mrs Oakland for being late. It doesn't really bother me though, as I'm usually late. I sit next to Chloe as usual, since it's part of the seating plan that our teacher has in place. She's fiddling with a pen again and I can't help but chuckle softly to myself. She's always doing that.

I then notice a bruise on her arm and frown. That was definitely not there earlier, I'm sure of it. When she catches me staring at it, Chloe covers it quickly with her hand, but I see her wince. It did look really bad, a deep purple colour. It's also pretty big, bigger than a £2 coin, so it's no wonder that it's so painful. "How did that happen?" I ask quietly, gesturing at the bruise she's covering. She turns to me with a frown and sighs, "I fell off my chair in the library and smacked my arm against the table." She huffs, "Honestly Chase, you worry too much."

But I have every right to worry, something's going on and I need to find out what!

~Chloe~

I know what you're thinking, why did I lie to Chase? Truthfully, I just couldn't tell him, I just couldn't! It was awful! After Kyle knocked me backwards, he grabbed me by the arm and began to twist it so much that it was a huge struggle trying to prevent myself from crying out. He left that bruise there.

Kyle is so horrible! You can see why I'm so scared of him. I was shouting, begging him to stop and that's when the librarian came over. Kyle let go of me pretty quickly then. The librarian, Miss Dickens, asked what was going on, but I couldn't say anything. I knew what would happen if I told her the truth, so I told her the same thing I told Chase: that I fell off my chair. But I told her that Kyle was just helping me up. She seemed to believe it and left us alone. Kyle immediately began twisting my arm again, this time so hard I felt like screaming. Screaming for a teacher to come, or Chase, or just...someone!

It was a huge relief when the bell went and he finally let me go. I scrambled up on my feet, grabbing my things before running to the classroom and sitting in my place.

When Chase came in, I couldn't bear to look at him, so I just stared at the whiteboard. The bruise hurt a lot when I tried to cover it, but I had to. Chase wouldn't stop staring at it. But there's nothing I can do about it. It's like this every day, so I always know what to expect at break or lunch. It's always the same thing and it feels like I'm in this endless cycle of pain and terror that no matter how hard I try, I just cannot escape!

Back to school, my first two lessons of the day were English and Maths. They were okay. Maths isn't my best subject but I love English. My favourite part is the creative writing side of it. During my spare time, I sometimes write scripts for plays or little skits that me, Chase and some of our friends like to act out together.

Coincidentally, my next lesson is Drama and it's honestly the best! Currently, we're working on some performances in small groups. Chase and I are with our friends Sophia and Carlos. I'm going to play the auntie, Carlos is a teenage boy that always gets into trouble (A bit like Chase, haha), Sophia is the niece and Chase is the grandad. Carlos was supposed to be the grandad but he kept complaining so we let him be the teenager.

We begin to act out the play and it's honestly so funny. Carlos suddenly grabs the walking stick that Chase was holding and says, "Allow me to assist you on your trip, grandpa!" He then proceeds to trip Chase up with the walking stick. Chase scowls, "You ain't no grandson of mine! Get back here you little rascal!" He gets up and begins chasing Carlos around the drama studio, waving the walking stick wildly. It's so funny that I burst out laughing.

But Kyle starts glaring at me, "What's the joke laughalot!" I instantly stop laughing, nibbling my lip nervously. Kyle frowns, "Oi! I said what's the joke? Answer me, you clown!" The whole class bursts out laughing, except for Chase. He folds his arms, narrowing his eyes at Kyle, "Don't call her names, Kyle." Kyle starts laughing, "Whoa! Chill Chase! I'm only joking! And it was pretty funny watching you chase Carlos around." Chase then starts laughing himself, "Yeah! It was!"

The bell then rings and we all gather our things. I then run off to my next class, P.E. Thankfully the girls are separate from the boys, which is a great relief. We have dance today, which is my favourite. I'm alright at most sports but I'm best at dance.

After getting changed into my P.E kit in the girls changing room, I head into the sports hall with the rest of the girls in the class. Miss Roseland is our P.E teacher and she's one of the best in the school. She's assigned us to come up with a routine in the style of our choice. So we're all rehearsing again. I like contemporary, ballet, hip hop and jazz, so I'm doing a fusion of all of them. The song I picked is called 'Stronger (What doesn't kill you.)' but I don't remember who it's by though.

I begin to dance, doing a bit of ballet and contemporary moves first. When it gets to the chorus, I spice it up, doing a combination of Jazz and Hip Hop moves. It's such a great song that I'm dancing to, and I'm so into the dance that I don't hear the bell go.

"Right guys! A few of you will be performing your own dance routines in the upcoming show." Miss Roseland tells us, "If I call out your name, then you will be required to find a song and costume as well as come up with an original routine for your dance." We all gather around as Miss Roseland gets ready to read out her list of names. I wonder who she is going to pick.

"The people who will be performing are as follows: Claire, Beth, Sarah and Chloe. Good luck to you all." She smiles at us all. *Wow! Me?! I didn't think I was that good.* As I smile with excitement, my classmates make their way out of the sports hall to go and get changed. But I decide to hang back to practise some more. Miss Roseland leaves the sports hall which means I'm by myself.

I head over to the computer by the sports cupboard and find the song I'm using. I begin playing the song and I start practising my routine. It starts out pretty well, but then I start getting this weird feeling that I'm being watched. And when I turn around, Kyle is there, smirking. *Oh no!* Within seconds, I felt his fist smash into my face. The impact is so strong that it sends me flying to the floor. "Pathetic little wretch!" He laughs, "You're absolutely rubbish at everything! You don't deserve to have been picked!"

And with that, he turns on his heel and leaves the room.

~Chase~

Chloe is late coming out of the sports hall but I soon find out why. Miss Roseland says she's staying behind to practise. I can hear music coming from the sports hall so I guess that makes sense. Well, she'll know where I'll be. In the canteen having my lunch of course! Today it's Tuna Pasta, mine and Chloe's favourite!

Heading to the canteen, I ponder over whether I should have waited for her or not. I'm really hungry though and I know Chloe won't mind. She'll just meet up with me later. I'd better eat now or I'll be very hungry later.

Choosing the tuna pasta, I have some garlic bread on the side, a bottle of pop to drink and a little cake for after. It comes to £4.50 but that's okay because I have a lot of money. After paying for my lunch, I sit at the table and tuck in. By the time I've finished, I get a lot more concerned. Chloe should have been here by now! Where is she?

After dealing with my tray, I go looking for Chloe. I check the sports hall, corridors, classrooms, the library, anywhere I can think of where Chloe may be. But to my dismay, I can't find her anywhere. One last place comes to mind so I make my way there. The girls changing rooms. Obviously, I can't go in there, cause I'm a boy. But I knock on the door.

1 in 100 – Living with Bipolar
Sometimes some of the girls in our class hang out there during lunch, so maybe Chloe is with them?

Within a few seconds, the door opens and Sophie walks out. "Hey, Chase. What's up?" "Is Chloe in there?" I ask, "She didn't meet me in the canteen for lunch." Sophie shakes her head, "No, she left a little while ago. Sorry." I nod, "Oh, okay, thanks." I then run off, looking for Chloe. I have a weird feeling about this. It's not like her to just disappear like this. Going back to the canteen, I check around there to see if Chloe is having her lunch but unfortunately she's not there. I then ask some of our classmates if they have seen her or know where she is. But every time it's a no. *Where could she be??*

Eventually, the bell rings for our last lesson of the day and I have to run. Our final lesson is Design and the classroom is on the opposite side of the school Great. Does that mean I'm late again? You betcha. Our teacher Mr Herring gives me a lecture about tardiness before letting me go to my seat. At the moment we're doing woodwork in design and the current project is making funky photo frames. Chloe and I were working together on ours. We went for a heart that has all these quirky spirals and flowers coming off of it. As well as a few lightning bolts. (My idea! Cool, right?) It's going to have a photo of our family in it and I think mum and dad are going to love it!

Chloe still hasn't shown up and it's really worrying me but I try my best to concentrate on our project. Though it is very fiddly and tricky by myself. With Chloe working on it too, there was always a spare hand to hold something in place or grip something if needed. I manage the best I can, but the whole time my mind is on Chloe. *Where are you, Chloe? What aren't you telling me? Why aren't you here? Are you okay?!*

Before I even know it, the bell rings for the end of school and there's a sudden blurred rush as everyone scrambles to pack everything away and gather their things so they can leave. Slowly I pack up my equipment and gather my things before making my way out of school and back home. The minute I get back, I run straight to mum. "Mum! Mum! Chloe's missing! She disappeared after P.E and I haven't seen her since!" Mum laughs lightly, "Don't be silly Chase! Chloe isn't missing! She came home at lunchtime since she wasn't feeling too good. Wearing sunglasses, would you believe?" I let out a huge sigh of relief, "Where is she?" I ask. Mum shrugs, "In her room, resting, I expect." I nod, "Okay! Thanks, mum!"

Running up the stairs, I begin calling her name. "Chloe!!" But there's no response and I frown in confusion. *I thought she was up here? She normally answers...so where is she?* Another thought then crosses my mind. *Hold up...she was wearing sunglasses? Inside??* Why would Chloe do that? Unless she's hiding something? I really need to find her now!

I check her bedroom but she's not there so I search everywhere upstairs before heading back down. Once downstairs, I check the living room and kitchen. Still no sign of Chloe. I begin to panic. *She's not run away, has she? Damn, what if she has? What do I do then? But where would she even go? None of this is making any sense!*

But right as I pass the cellar door, I hear a small sob. Quickly I scoot backwards and press my ear against the door. I hear someone crying. That has to be Chloe! Immediately, I open the door and slip inside. The cellar isn't very big, almost like a little box room, but you can still walk around in it a little. As I go down the steps, I see her sitting on the floor with her knees tucked up to her chin and her head is down.

Giving out another sigh of relief, I head over to her. "Chloe? Why are you hiding? What's wrong?" She shakes her head, not saying a word and sobs harder. So I put my hands on her shoulders and face her, "Chloe, look at me. I know you're hiding something. But you can tell me, you can tell me anything! You know that!" I say. But there's no response and I sigh, "Chloe, please talk to me. I'm really worried about you. We've never kept anything from each other before. So why should this be any different?"

Chloe then lifts up her head and looks me straight in the eye. I gasp in shock and horror at what I'm seeing. Tears slide down her cheeks. One eye is red and puffy from crying and the other... well...it's purple and black, very clearly badly bruised. "Someone did this to you, didn't they? Who was it?" Chloe shakes her head, refusing to speak. I frown, "Chloe...who did this to you? Please! Just tell me! Who the hell did it?" Chloe sniffs, "K-kyle...he did it. He does it sometimes. This is the first time it was in the face though." My eyes widen in horror, "What do you mean sometimes?! How long has this been going on for?" Chloe bites her lip nervously, "Ever since we moved to this school in the middle of year eight. He's been hitting me, pushing me around and hurting me non stop. And the things he says… I just feel so worthless and pathetic."

"Chloe, you're far from either of those things. You don't deserve any of this!" I say, taking my hands off of her shoulders and clenching my fists in anger. How dare Kyle do this to my sister! He will pay for this! No one hurts my sister and gets away with it. But it all makes sense now. She must have gone to the medical room at lunchtime and the nurse must have sent her home because it's so bad. It also explains why she always seems so afraid when we walk to school in the mornings. And why she's seemed so distant and down lately. How did I not realise it sooner! I knew something was up! I should have seen it! I should have known it was something like bullying.

"I'm so sorry Chase."

Frowning, I look at Chloe in confusion. "What on earth for?" Tears pour down her face. "For lying about the bruises and for keeping all of this from you. I-i just didn't know how and...i-i thought you might not believe me." I raise an eyebrow, "Why would you think I wouldn't believe you? I can always tell when you're telling the truth, remember?" She shrugs, "Yes but...well...wasn't Kyle one of your friends?" I shake my head, "I mean I guess maybe at first, but you're my sister, my twin! Of course, I'd believe you! And you're being bullied for crying out loud! You'd have to be crazy to lie about something as bad as that!" I then smile, "Hey, don't dwell on it too much. At least you told me now. Which means we can deal with it and get it to stop! Don't you worry sis! I have your back! Always!"

For the first time in what feels like forever, Chloe gives me a genuine smile. "Thanks, Chase."

~Chloe~

I'm so glad I told Chase about all of this. It's honestly such a relief. It's like a huge weight has been lifted off of my shoulders and I don't feel so alone anymore. Chase then nudges me, "Hey, I heard you got picked to dance in the school show. That's awesome!" I just shrug. "I don't think I want to do the show anymore. I'll only mess it all up and end up a laughing stock. I'm useless." Chase's eyes widen and he frowns, "Did *he* tell you that? Chloe just ignore him! Don't listen to a single filthy word that comes out of that guy's mouth. He's only jealous cause he can't dance. I mean he has two left feet. Besides, Miss Roseland must think you're an excellent dancer, which is why she picked you. And I agree with her! You're the best dancer at the school! I'm your brother, better yet your twin! You know that you can take my word on that!"

I smile softly, "Thanks, Chase!" I then hug him gratefully. This is why he's my best friend! I honestly don't know what I would do without him sometimes. Whilst we're sitting on the cellar floor, we chat away and he keeps cracking all these terrible jokes. But it makes me smile and really cheers me up. Sometime later we hear mum calling us for dinner so we both race each other up the cellar stairs and into the dining room to eat.

After dinner, which was shepherds pie and utterly delicious, we do our homework and then just hang out for a while. Eventually, it is time for bed and as I snuggle under my warm duvet and gaze up at the dark ceiling above me, tears slide down my cheeks. Thousands of thoughts circle around my head, making it very difficult for me to fall asleep! *I wish Kyle would leave me alone! I don't know how much more I can take! What is he going to do next? How is it ever going to get better, when every day gets, even worse than the last? What if he finds out I told someone?! What is he going to do to me? Maybe I shouldn't have told Chase. What if Kyle starts on him next? What if they fight? What if Chase gets hurt? What should I do?!!!*
After several hours of trying to shut out the thoughts in my head, my eyes drop and I finally fall asleep.

"Chloe?"

"Chloe! Wake up!"

I open my eyes slowly and groan. The first thing I see is Chase shaking me awake. "What?" I mumble. "We're gonna be late for school if you don't get up!" Rolling my eyes, I turn away from him, "I'm not going." I hear him scoff, "Come on, you have to! It's literally the law." I shrug, "I don't feel well, okay? And anyway, why do you care so much about school? You're literally never on time for anything!" Chase shrugs, "Yeah, yeah, I know. But I'm not gonna risk getting grounded for skipping school. And you shouldn't either." "I won't say it again, I'm not going!" I snap and

Chase sighs, sitting on the end of the bed. "This is about Kyle, isn't it? Look, I know you're scared, but I promise I won't let him hurt you." I poke my head out of the duvet curiously, "You mean that? But how exactly?" Chase sighs, "Well that's easy. I won't let him near you. If we all stay in a group, you, me and all our friends won't dare try anything. Trust me. And of course, I mean it! A promise is a promise!"

Pondering over this, I hesitate but when I look up at Chase, I nod. He's the person I trust the most and I know he wouldn't ever let me down. Slowly, I sit up and I nod. "Okay." He grins, "Right then! Hurry up and get ready! I wasn't kidding when I said we were gonna be late!" I laugh, shaking my head at him as he heads out. I rush around getting ready, making sure to cover my bruises with makeup, before heading out the front door with Chase, on our way to school.

As we walk into the school playground, I see Kyle smirking at me, his eyes gleaming. But Chase also notices and gently pulls me away and out of Kyle's line of sight. As we continue walking, I see Chase glare at Kyle. He's usually pretty protective of me but I know my brother, this isn't just being protective, I can tell he also wants revenge. I frown at Chase for a second as we reach the other side of the playground. Carlos and Joe then come running up to us. Carlos grins at me, "Hey Chloe! What's up?" He then turns to Chase, "Hey what's happening, bro?" The three boys then do this weird handshake, whilst I shake my head at them, chuckling. They look so silly!

"BOO!"

I shriek, jumping with fright as the person that snuck up behind me grabs my shoulders. I then hear everyone laughing and turn to see Sophia standing there, doubled over with laughter. I roll my eyes and laugh as well. "Nice one Sophia!" Chase says. Sophia beams, "Haha, thanks. And sorry Clo, I couldn't resist!" I smile, "Hey, it's fine Soph, but I'll get you back for that!" "Bring it!" Sophia laughs. As we all compose ourselves, Chase turns to the group. " So I was thinking we should all hang out together from now on, like a proper squad!" "Brilliant idea!" Sophia cheers and everyone nods in agreement.

Suddenly the bell rings and we all rush off to class. And for once, Chase is actually on time! As we sit down at our table, I see Kyle glaring. He really doesn't like that he can't get to me. For me though, it feels pretty great. Maybe things will be better now? I guess we'll just have to see.

A few weeks later…

~Chase~

We've been hanging out so much lately, thanks to my brilliant idea! The best part is that Chloe is safe and Kyle can't get to her. He really doesn't like it, but who cares? It's much better this way and now Chloe is starting to be much happier and less afraid when we go to school.

It's another usual day at school and we've finished our first few lessons of the day. It's now break time and I'm packing up my things so I can head out and join the others. But that's

when Kyle walks up to me. "Still trying to protect your sister, are you? Well, we know that won't last!" I just ignore him and finish sorting my things. Kyle then scoffs, "She's such a baby! Always depending on her to save the day all the time! Even though she knows he can't always be there to protect her. Pathetic little baby, ha!" A surge of anger boils over me and I grab him by his shirt, having had enough of him. "Don't you dare hurt her again! If you ever come even close to her, I will beat you so badly until you can't stand it! Do you get me? SO LEAVE HER ALONE!" I shout and he laughs in my face. Immediately I clench my fist and get ready to punch him. He is so going to get it!

"Chase!"

As soon as I hear her voice, I stop in my tracks. Feeling her gently tugging at my arm, I turn to her in surprise. When I look at her, I see the frightened look on her face as she shakes her head. Sighing, I reluctantly let Kyle go and he runs off. I let my arms drop defeatedly. My sister always seems to know when I'm about to do something stupid and knows how to talk me out of it, even without saying a word. Chloe then grabs my arm and leads me outside. I can tell that she's going to give me a talking to and if I try to struggle it would only make it worse. So I do nothing and let her lead me to the cluster of trees on one side of the sports field. We call it the woodland area and it's our private go-to spot if we need to have a twin talk.

As we get there, she turns to me with a frown. "Chase, you're not just trying to protect me, are you? I can tell." I remain silent and she sighs, "You want revenge on Kyle, for hurting me. Chase, that's wrong! You shouldn't get your own back on someone just because they've done something bad to you or someone you care about. Two wrongs don't make a right!" I hang my head in shame and sigh, "I know, I know! It's just...I can't stand him calling you names and hurting you. It makes me so angry. I just want to wipe that smug grin off of his ugly face!" Chloe shakes her head at me but then smiles, "Well if we keep hanging out in our squad, he can't can he? I mean it's worked so far, right?" I nod slowly, "I guess you're right." Chloe laughs, "Okay then! Now, how's about a twin hug?" I chuckle and nod, "Sure!" I then hug her and we laugh before heading to find our squad. I wonder where they've gotten to?

~Chloe~

When we find the squad, we hang out with them for the remainder of break time. When the bell goes we head to our next class, which happens to be french. Today's lesson is going to be pretty fun. Once a month, our teacher either brings in some french food or teaches us how to make the dish. Today it's the classic crepes. We're working in pairs and naturally, I'm with Chase. We've got our crepe pans on the go and the whole classroom is starting to smell amazing! Everything is going great!

Miss Allaire - our french teacher - then realises that she left the plates in the canteen's kitchen, so she sends me to get them. As I leave the classroom I hear her ask someone else to help but I don't catch the name. I continue making my way to the canteen.

When I get there, I head into the kitchen and pick up the stack of plates. That's when I feel a hard tap on my shoulder. Realising it's probably the other person, I put the plate down and turn to them to see what's wrong. But my eyes quickly widen in fear when I see Kyle standing there in front of me. I then catch a glimpse of a shiny object in his hands and my heart starts pounding with panic as I freeze in fear. *He's got a knife!! And I'm trapped in the corner of the kitchen!* Within seconds, he lashes out with the knife. I try to move out of the way but I'm not quick enough. The knife catches me right across the face. I yelp and clutch my face, feeling blood dripping down. I stare at him in shock, I never thought he'd go this far!

Kyle smirks evilly, "Aw, did I mess up your little baby face? Thought it would be an improvement but you're even more ugly than before! And we can't have anyone else's eyes damaged by this ugliness, can we? But I can fix that!" He lunges at me again but this time I'm quicker and manage to dodge out of the way. Kyle scowls and repeatedly tries to hit me with the knife but he keeps missing as the adrenaline within me lets me gain enough strength to get out of the way.

But then I trip over and fall backwards, landing on my back. Kyle's eyes gleam as he comes at me. I'm unable to move and look around frantically, trying to come up with an idea. But nothing comes to mind and I realise there's only one possible thing I can do. I don't know if anyone will hear, but it's the only option I have left and I have to try!

I let out an ear-piercing scream, screaming as loud as I can and stretching it out as much as I can between breaths. It could echo through the corridors and run into all the classrooms but will *he* hear? *Please, Chase, hear me!*

Kyle has backed off a little, covering his ears. I guess my screaming is hurting him a bit. But he looks really annoyed and is shaking his head in frustration. But then he rapidly darts forward, clamping his hand over my mouth so I can no longer scream. He gives me an evil menacing look and I whimper with fright.

He's going to kill me. I just know he is.

~Chase~

I'm making my way to the school canteen. Miss Allaire sent me to help Chloe and Kyle. Honestly, I'm kind've glad, I don't trust Kyle around my sister. He'll use every opportunity he can to hurt her, so right now I can't help but worry. And as I'm walking down the corridor, my worries rapidly increase to straight panic when a blood-curdling scream tears through the air. *Oh no! This is really bad!*

"Chloe!" I cry out and bolt towards the canteen, but as I get there the screams stop and my mind begins racing. *Please tell me I'm not too late! Come on Chase, get a move on!* Rapidly, I burst into the kitchen and within a split second, grab hold of Kyle. "HOW DARE YOU HURT HER!" I yell and throw him into the unit. He smacks into the cupboards with a bang and a knife drops from his hands. It slides across the floor and I hastily pick it up.

Instantly I notice blood on it and my eyes widen in horror. My attention goes straight to Chloe. Putting the knife out of reach, I head over to her side. Chloe is hunched up in a corner, her face buried in her hands. She's crying and her body is shaking very violently. Crouching down next to her, I put my arms around. "It's okay. I'm here. It's okay Chloe. You're safe now." She sobs into my shoulder but then whimpers with pain, lifting her head. My eyes widen in horror at the blood on her face, coming from a large cut. I grab some kitchen roll and try to hold it on the wound, all the while keeping my eye on Kyle. But fortunately, he doesn't seem to be doing anything. He sat on the floor, groaning. Guess that collision took the wind out of him.

A teacher then walks in and looks around the room in shock. She probably heard the screaming and all the commotion. She looks at Kyle and then at me and Chloe. "What on earth is going on here?!" Kyle immediately glares at me. "He attacked me! And then his sister! He's a psycho! He should be expelled!" The teacher turns to me with a frown, "Is this true?" I shake my head, "Absolutely not! I'd never ever hurt Chloe! I heard her screaming when I was on my way down here. Cause Kyle attacked my sister! Slashed her across the face with a knife! All I did was pull him away from her and put the knife out of reach before trying to help Chloe." To my surprise, Chloe then speaks up. "Chase is telling the truth. He slammed Kyle into the unit but it was to protect me. Kyle's been bullying me since I started at this school, calling me horrible names and beating me black and blue. I was too afraid of him, too scared to say anything, until now."

The teacher nods and takes out her two-way radio. We hear her talking to someone and a few minutes later members of the behaviour team, along with the headmaster and the deputy. The members of the behaviour team take hold of Kyle and haul him up, keeping him restrained. "Take him to my office. I'll deal with him later." The headmaster says and the behaviour team take Kyle away. A teacher then comes over to us and inspects Chloe's injuries. "I think our best bet is to take you up to A&E. Chase, if you could go and gather your sister's things and meet us up in reception, that would be appreciated. We'll inform your parents while we're there." I nod, "Yes miss! But if it's okay, I'd like to go with Chloe." The teacher nods, "Very well. But don't dilly dally will you? Another teacher will accompany you and explain to Miss Allaire."

I nod again and rush up to the classroom, closely followed by a teacher. Once there I gather mine and Chloe's things before heading up to reception to be with my sister. She's sat on a chair, holding a cloth to her face. Seeing a few stray tears down her face, I realise it's starting to sink in what happened. I sit beside her with my arm around her, our school bags at our feet, as we listen to the teacher talking on the phone. A little while later the teacher comes back and tells us that our parents will meet us at the hospital. She then begins walking us to her car. Because of how small the teacher's car park is, there's an allocated section across the road for them to park, which is where we happened to be headed.

As we're about to cross the road, we hear footsteps storming after us. Glancing over my shoulder, my eyes widen seeing that it is Kyle. He snarls at me with a murderous look in his eyes. "YOU LIAR! HOW DARE YOU! YOU'RE GONNA PAY FOR THIS! I'LL...I'LL KILL YOU!" The next few moments are a blur as he charges at me and shoves me hard in the direction of the road. There's a loud screech and waves of agony jolt through my body as everything rapidly goes black.

~Chloe~

My eyes widen in horror as I see the car hit Chase and send him flying. He hits the ground with such force and he remains unmoving. "CHASE!" I scream and I run over to him. Kneeling beside him, I see that his eyes are shut tight, grazes cover his hands and blood trickles down his face. Tears pour furiously down my face as I look up at Kyle in anger. He's being restrained by the headmaster, who must've run after him. He's pretty strong so Kyle isn't going anywhere. Feeling my blood boil I glare at Kyle fiercely, unafraid for the first time. "How could you!?! Didn't you think you'd done enough already?!" I gesture at the still bleeding wound on my face. "Don't you think you've hurt me enough?! If Chase dies, I'll never forgive you! And I'm gonna make sure you pay for this! I SWEAR TO GOD I'M GOING TO GET YOU BEHIND BARS FOR THE REST OF YOUR LIFE IF IT'S THE LAST THING I DO!" I scream at him.

But I then turn my attention back to Chase. It doesn't matter how angry I am with Kyle. Chase comes first. Tears pour down my face as I sob uncontrollably. *He's in such a bad way! What if he does die? What will I do then? I can't lose him! He's my twin! My best friend! I can't live without him!* The driver of the car has joined us and he's also in a mess. "I-i'm so sorry! I didn't see him! H-he came out of nowhere! I tried to stop!" I look up at him, "He didn't run out on purpose! He was pushed! By that guy over there that is currently being restrained! He pushed my brother! He tried to kill him! We need police as well as an ambulance." The driver looks very shocked but he nods. "I already called an ambulance but I'll call back to get the police." I nod before lowering my head as I try, looking down at Chase. The teacher that was with us is kneeling down next to me and trying to do some first aid. A little while later an ambulance arrives and the paramedics immediately rush over. One of them tries to pry me away from Chase but the other one shakes her head. "Just let the girl stay. It's clear they're very close and besides she's hardly in the way is she?" The first paramedic shakes his head and they both tend to Chase.

A teacher comes up to me and tells me that she's going to call my parents to let them know what has happened. But it doesn't fully register. My mind is solely on Chase and nothing will shake it. The second paramedic keeps asking me questions but I can't focus on what she's saying, nor am I able to speak. I manage to stammer out our names but that is all. Chase is taken into the ambulance and one of the paramedics leads me there as well and while she monitors Chase, she also gives my injury a quick look over. Once she's done, I spend the rest of the journey to the hospital holding Chase's hand.

When we arrive, Chase is whisked away to the emergency unit while I'm taken to a cubicle in the minor injuries unit. A doctor then comes in and examines me before applying stitches to the wound on my face. Afterwards, I'm taken to a waiting area in the emergency unit. A kind nurse gives me a drink of water as I sit down but even though my mouth is so dry, I'm unable to take a sip. My hands are trembling as I stare down at the water in my cup, thousands of thoughts flooding my mind. *Will he make it? What if he doesn't make it? What will I do? Why did this have to happen? And why Chase? Why does this have to happen to him?!*

A short while later my parents arrive and they immediately bombard me with a lot of questions. What happened to me? What happened to Chase? Who did this? Why didn't I tell them I was being bullied? How is Chase doing? Have I heard anything? But I'm still so in shock that I can barely speak at all and tears spill down my face yet again. Mum puts her arms around me and Dad sits beside us, supporting us. It's not long before a doctor comes over and informs us that Chase needs to be taken into surgery. The doctor explains the surgery and potential risks. Dad then sorts the paperwork and after that, it's a long, agonising wait.

Several hours pass and we've yet to hear anything. Mum did a food run but I'm too scared and worried to eat. Both of my parents keep asking if I need or want anything but the only thing I want is to know that Chase is okay. And with every minute that passes, the more worried I get. I keep trying to convince myself that it's just some crazy nightmare. That I'll wake up any second and it will be okay. Chase will be right there smiling and laughing like he usually does. But it's not a dream and as time goes on, the more I fear that I'm going to lose my brother.

Finally after what feels like forever, a doctor approaches and my parents instantly rise to their feet. I go to get up too, but the doctor insists on speaking to my parents privately in his office. This means I'm left in the waiting room by myself, left to assume the worst. By the time my parents get back, I'm practically sobbing. A nurse is trying to calm me down but it's clearly not working. Mum rushes over and hugs me. "He's dead isn't he?" I howl and mum shakes her head, comforting me, "No honey, no. Your brother is still with us. The operation went well. But I'm afraid he's got a long fight ahead of him." I look up at her in confusion, "W-what do you mean?" She sits me down gently. "While the surgery went well, there were some complications." "Complications?" I ask quizzically. My mum sighs, "Chloe....your brother...h-he slipped into a coma. But they don't know when...or even if he'll wake up. But Chase is a fighter, you know that, so don't give up hope okay?" I nod slowly, trying to take it all in but it's a struggle to process.

"I want to see him," I say. "I want to see Chase!" Mum and Dad exchange hesitant glances and after a few seconds, reluctantly nod, sighing. They lead me around some corridors and into a room on the ICU ward. My heart shatters seeing the state Chase is in. Bruised and cut up, wires all around him. An unsettling silence hits the room, a heart monitor beeping and a ventilator breathing air into my brother's lungs are the only sounds. Shakily, I made my way to the chair at his bedside. As I sit down, I gently take hold of his hand. "I'm here Chase." I say, "I'm right here, okay? And I will be, every day! I promise!" I gently hook my little finger around his bruised one. "That's a twin promise!"   I then feel a hand on my shoulder, "Come on Chloe. Time to go home." Mum says and I shake my head, "No! Not yet!" She frowns, "Chloe, we have to. The doctors have to monitor him carefully. The first 24 hours are critical. You'll see him again tomorrow. Don't worry." "But…" I trail off, seeing the look on her face and realising it's pointless to argue. Reluctantly I let go of Chase's hand and follow them out of the room. We then head home.

The following day, mum takes me to the hospital to see Chase. Once again, I sit by his bedside and hold his hand. Not really knowing what to do, I start to chat to him softly. *Maybe he can hear me? I hope so.* A short time later, mum leaves the room to get herself a coffee. Glancing at Chase once more, I sigh. "I miss you so much, Chase. I don't know

what to do. Whenever I've gone through something or have been sad, you were always right there, but now...now I don't have you here and I don't know if I can do it." I sniff, wiping my eyes. "But I guess...I guess I have to try. You'd want me to be strong, right Chase? So I'll try, okay? For you, I'll try to be strong." Wiping my eyes I take a deep breath before starting to sing softly to him. Singing is something Chase and I loved to do. Whether it'd be along to a song on the radio or karaoke, we'd always be singing together. But when Kyle started bullying me, I stopped because of how much he made fun of it in the beginning. So it's been a while. But I feel that Chase would like it, so I'm singing to him. And I actually get so absorbed in it that I don't hear mum walk back in.

"Chloe! Stop that! You know there's no point! Chase can't hear you!"

Startled, I look at her in bewilderment. "W-what? What do you mean?" She sighs, "Well how can he hear you? Look at the state he's in. I know you mean well but you're just going to upset yourself more and be disappointed. I think you should just leave it." Right at that moment, a doctor walks in and he shakes his head in disagreement. "Actually coma patients' brains can process things in the environment around them. Like footsteps or the sound of someone's voice. Studies have even shown that familiar music can probably increase arousal in patients and enhance their cognitive processes. So your daughter's singing may help him become more aware of things and maybe even help bring him out of the coma. Especially if they used to sing together or he used to enjoy hearing her sing. Though only time will tell if there will be any improvement and obviously nothing is certain or guaranteed. But her singing won't cause any harm. If she wants to do that, she may."

And that is exactly what I do. Over the several months that follow, every time I visit Chase, I sing to him. I don't know if it is helping at all but I know deep down he hears me. He's there. He has to be. I miss him so much. Initially, I kept going to his room to wake him up each morning, as I'd always used to do, only to find it empty and gathering dust. It took me at least a week to get out of that habit. But still every morning, I come down to the breakfast table and find myself constantly staring at his empty seat, imagining him sitting there with a big sleepy grin and crumbs all over his face. My journey to school is lonely without him there to talk to. Everyone always asks about him, about how he's doing. But I never have anything new to tell them. He's got a bunch of get well soon cards from all our classmates. Chase was pretty popular with everyone and that's because of how kind and friendly he was. I don't think there was anyone here that didn't like him.

It's hard to focus on school. I try my best to concentrate on the lessons but my mind always drifts back to Chase. The empty seat next to me, where he used to sit, is a constant reminder that he's not here. That he's stuck in the hospital, still fighting for his life. It's so hard not to just start crying every time I see that empty chair. I still have our squad, our friends. But even though I have them for company, I still feel so lonely and alone. The squad isn't the same. Not without Chase's terrible jokes, his laugh, his smile. He made things so much more lively. Now there's just a Chase shaped piece missing from it. I can tell the others think the same but they're trying their best to keep things light and cheery. They're all really supportive too, which means a lot to me. I also don't have to worry about

Kyle anymore. He's locked up now and there's going to be a huge trial at court. I'll have to give evidence, which is something I'm not looking forward to because it means having to recall all the details of the traumatic events that happened. But I need to get justice for Chase.

My parents are also making me see a therapist to help me deal with everything that has been going on. I guess they were worried about how withdrawn I've become and that I don't always feel like eating. And how hard it is to sleep at night. No matter how hard I try, I'll never be able to forget what happened that day. It replays on my mind constantly, stuck like a broken record. It's so much worse at night time though, I get these horrible nightmares that keep me awake most of the night and cause me to have panic attacks. My therapist suggested I start writing. She thinks it will help me express myself and everything that I'm feeling or worrying about and maybe even help me cope with everything that has happened.

I guess the good thing is that my injuries have healed and I no longer have stitches. But thanks to Kyle, I may now be permanently disfigured. My therapist keeps telling me that I'm not disfigured, it's just a small scar that still could heal. She also is encouraging me to not see it as an ugly reminder of that day, but rather a reminder of strength and courage, of how I endured through tough times and the warrior that is within me. I don't know if I believe that, but I'm trying to. I don't feel strong at all though. The more time that goes on, the harder it gets and the more I feel that I'll lose Chase completely. The doctors keep trying to convince us to pull the plug on him. They don't believe he'll get better and think that turning off his life support is the best thing for him as it's essentially ending his suffering. Mum and Dad are constantly refusing, trying to give Chase more time to come back to us. But lately, even they are losing faith and I keep begging them to wait a little longer before 'pulling the plug'. I'm really scared though. I don't know how long I can keep this up. I know I'm only on borrowed time and won't be able to keep stalling them for long. But I just can't do it! I can't let Chase go! How can I? I'm probably the only one of us who has any hope left, I still have faith in him! I can't give up on him. Not yet!

Another month passes by and there is still no improvement. The thought that I'll be forced to let Chase go is terrifying me. But with how things have been going, turning off Chase's life support may be imminent. As we head up to the hospital, I get this nagging feeling in the back of my mind, a vast wave of uneasiness in the pit of my stomach. Mum and Dad are both with me today which is unusual as Dad works most of the time and tries to visit Chase when he is able - which isn't very often. So something feels very off to me and it's adding to the uneasiness I'm feeling.

When we reach Chase's room, I'm made to wait outside while Mum and Dad spend time with him. *What's going on here?* Normally we go in together at first and later on I get one on one time with my brother. *Something feels wrong.* Mum and Dad also looked pretty sad when they went in, a lot sadder than usual. *Do they know something? Are they keeping something from me? But why? What is going on?!*

After around twenty minutes, Mum and Dad emerge from Chase's room. They exchange sorrowful glances before nodding at each other. I frown, "Can I go in and see Chase now?"

Mum sighs, "Actually before you do, we need to have a talk." Confused, I tilt my head at her quizzically, "About what? What's going on?" Mum sits be down next to her and gives me a sympathetic look. "Chloe, sweetheart...I know this is something you're not going to want to hear but your Dad and I...well we both agree that it's time." "Time for what? I don't understand." I ask and she puts her arm around me and places her hand over mine. "I know this is going to be really hard for you to accept, but it's time for you to say your goodbyes to Chase." My eyes widen in shock as the truth dawns in on me and I stare at her in disbelief. "Say goodbye?! Y-you're pulling the plug on him?! Turning off his life support?! Y-you can't!" I stammer and Dad frowns, "Chloe, don't make this harder than it is. The doctors believe this is the best thing for Chase. He hasn't shown any improvement at all and he's not going to get any better. You don't want your brother to keep suffering, do you?"

Tears splash down my cheeks, knowing deep down what he's saying is true, but I shake my head, "No! He still could come back to us! People have been in comas for years and have still woken up! Chase still has a chance! We can't give up on him!" "Chloe, your Dad is right. And we don't want to let Chase go any more than you do, but based on the results from his last few assessments...well you know that he regressed into PVS. You remember what that is?" I nod, "Persistive Vegetative State. I know. But people can still recover from that! Please! Don't pull the plug yet, I'm begging you. Please! Not yet!" Tears are pouring down my face as I look at them both pleadingly. Mum shakes her head, "You know as well as I do that we've been holding it off for long enough. Please, just go and say your goodbyes to your brother and spend some time with him. He'd want you to be with him in his last moments. You are his twin after all." As I glance at my parents and see the expressions on their faces, I know it's pointless to protest any further. I look them both in the eyes, "Fine. But just because you've given up on him, it doesn't mean I have, that's something I could never do. You're making a huge mistake! I just know it!"

I turn on my heel and walk into Chase's room. But as soon as I shut the door, I flop down in the seat at his bedside and start sobbing. "It's not fair! Why does this have to happen?! I can't lose you, Chase! You're my twin brother! My best friend! How am I supposed to function without you?! They can't pull the plug on you, we all still need you! I need you!" I hold Chase's hand and squeeze it hard as I cry. "You have to come back to us, Chase! Time is running out! You know I'd never give up on you but they all want to pull the plug on you. They don't think you'll get better and that this is for the best! But they're wrong! They have to be! You wouldn't leave me, would you Chase? Come on, please! Please wake up, I beg you! Prove them wrong! Just come back to us, Chase!" *Come back to me!*

The door then creaks open and as I look over I see Mum and Dad walk in, followed by some doctors. My heart instantly sinks as mum gives me a sympathetic look. "Sweetheart...it's time." My eyes widen as I suddenly snap. "NO!" I quickly position myself between them and Chase, blocking them from getting to him. Mum sighs sadly, "Chloe come on, please don't do this. Not now. Don't make this harder than it has to be. You need to let him go." I shake my head furiously and tears stream down my face as I put my arm around Chase. "NO! I WON'T LET HIM GO! I WON'T LET YOU DO THIS!" "Chloe stop this nonsense!" Dad snaps. "This is what is best for your brother and not up for debate!" One of the doctors turns to me, "Listen, little one. I know this is hard for you. I see how much you love your brother but your Dad is right. This is the best thing

for him. Your brother will be in a better place and won't be suffering anymore. You love and care for him very much but sometimes in life if we love someone, we have to let them go. Now you're going to be a big brave girl right? For your brother?" I remain silent and seemingly satisfied with this, they turn to my parents, talking them through what to expect and they begin preparing.

My body moves of its own accord, setting into panic mode and hug Chase and even shaking him slightly as the tears keep flowing down my face as I scream. "CHASE! WAKE UP PLEASE! PLEASE CHASE! I CAN'T DO THIS WITHOUT YOU! WAKE UP, I'M BEGGING YOU!" A doctor tries to pry me away but I refuse to budge. Mum then tries to pull me away but I struggle ferociously. Another doctor tries to help but my adrenaline kicks in and I cling onto Chase with all of my might, my feet firmly planted to the ground. "NO! NO! YOU CAN'T! NO! CHASE!

CHASE PLEASE! PLEASE WAKE UP! NO-" I've suddenly yanked away and I scream with all of my might, using all the air in my lungs.

"CHASE!!!!"

~Chase~

Darkness all around me. I can't see anything, nor can I move. All I can do is hear. I hear what goes on around me. The squeak of wheels on a polished floor, the creak of a door opening and shutting. Weird beeping noises and the clacking of heels walking along the ground. There are voices all around me but they're all muffled and blurred. But I can pick one voice. I'd know it anywhere. *Chloe.*

Trapped in this darkness, I have no sense of time but what I do know is that she is always here. She talks to me, sings to me with her sweet voice. I imagine she's holding my hand all this time and I long to be able to reach out and squeeze her hand back. To let her know I'm still here. *I'm still here. Don't give up on me.* I keep trying to open my eyes, so I can see her face but they won't budge. It's like they're stuck with superglue and have a 100kg weight pressing down on them. It feels like I have a huge 1-ton weight pinning my body in place. I try with all my strength to fight it. So much pain is running through me. Waves of agony hit me again and again like the sea crashing against the cliffs. *Why can't I wake up? I wake up every morning with no problem, so why is this so hard? Why does this hurt so much? Why can't I move?!* I feel so stiff, like a wooden plank. I just want to move! I want to say something or call out to them. But I can't! *What is wrong with me?! Why can't I do anything?!*

I keep fighting, trying the best I can to do something. But the more I fight, the heavier my body becomes and the more exhausted and weaker I feel. *What is happening to me?!* It's becoming a real struggle to keep fighting. It's like something is sucking the energy from me, stealing my life force. I can feel something pulling me. I feel this glowing light around me. Flashes ignite and memories are scattered out in front of me. *Back at preschool, when a kid took Chloe's hat and threw it on top of the trike shed, I climbed all the way onto the roof to get the hat back. I fell off and broke my arm, but I got it back and also pushed that mean kid over. Then Disney trip, when we got to meet all our favourite characters and went*

on a bunch of cool rides! When we started high school and we had this huge group of friends and had a massive sleepover party and Chloe and I played a ton of pranks on them. When we had to move to a new school across the other side of the country because of Dad's work. We stuck together like glue, even when we found the friends we have now.

Why are all these memories suddenly springing up before me? And what is this light? What's going on? Am i....am I dying? Is this what it means to have your life flash before your eyes? But mine's only just begun! This can't...be it...right? No...I can already feel myself slipping. Is this really it? It's over? Already? This is how it ends? But what about school? What about my career? My hopes and dreams? *I wanted to be an astronaut. Or work at NASA. That would have been so cool!* And what about my friends? *Cole and Joe? We were going to throw some mad parties when we started college. And pick up the best girls! Not to mention buy and show off our first cars when we got the chance. Drive out to see some insane gigs and go on road trips.*

Then there's my family. My parents. They're never going to see their son grow up and become successful. Or see me have my own family one day. They'll never get to see me graduate, or start my new job in my dream profession, *And believe me, I definitely would've gotten there. I don't want to brag, but I'm very smart. Straight A's all around.* But finally, there's Chloe. *Chloe.* My sister, twin and best friend rolled into one. It's going to break her. But she's strong, she'll get there. She's way stronger than she could ever know. But I'll never get to see her become the superstar that she is. She could go on the west end, or be a backing dancer for a world-famous popstar, or even become the famous popstar herself. She could do it! *She's super smart too, so she could be anything and everything.. An astronaut, scientist, engineer, writer, popstar, whatever. She can be whatever she wants to be and I know she can do it!*

As my body continues to get weaker and my heart starts to slow, it sinks in that this is it. I'm dying and I can't stop it. It's all over. I wish that I didn't have to leave them all like this - leave Chloe like this. It's so unfair. Why did my life have to be so short? Why did- wait! Wait! No! This can't be it! No! I can't go now! I have so much planned in my life. So much left to do! And I can't leave Chloe! She needs me! And I need her! No! This is not it! I have to fight this! I have to fight this! *Come on Chase! You can do this! You can't give up now! They're counting on you!* With every ounce of energy and strength left in my body, I begin to fight the hardest I've ever fought in my entire life. *Come on Chase! You can beat this! Come on Chase! Wake up! Damn it, wake up will you? Wake up, Chase! WAKE UP!*

"His eyes are twitching! He's still there!"

"Don't be silly Chloe, it's just your imagination."

"No! They really did twitch!"

"Chloe…"

"They really did twitch! Please believe me! And it has to mean something! He's still there!"

"Stop this! It's just a reflex. Just let him go! The doctors are turning off the machines now. It's time to say goodbye!"

A blinding light hits my face as I finally feel my eyelids starting to lift. Everything is a hazy blur but the muffled voices I was used to hearing are becoming clearer. "No! You can't turn them off yet. This is a sign! We can't give up on him now! There's still a chance!" *Chloe. No matter how hopeless it seems, she still refuses to give up. This is why she is so strong.*

I'm struggling to open my eyes properly, there's only a tiny slit of light coming through. But I'm already starting to get some feeling back and that's how I know Chloe is gripping tightly on my hand. Mustering up a bit more strength, I try to squeeze as hard as I can, I don't know if it will work, but it's worth a try. Suddenly I hear her gasp. "Chase…?" *Did it work?* Her grip on my hand suddenly disappears but I hear a commotion. "Stop! Don't turn that off! Please! Just- just look at my brother first! Please? He is still there! He's still fighting!" I think that's to a doctor that was… that was going to turn off….my life support? *I guess it was really bad then. But since it's still on, the doctor must've listened and even if only for a moment, it's given me a chance.* "Chloe, stop this nonsense!" That sounds like Dad. "It's not nonsense! He just squeezed my hand! It was quite light but…" Her voice trails off and as my eyes start opening properly, I see her silhouette in front of me and she begins to speak again. "C-chase?! Oh my god! Mum, Dad! Look!"

As my eyes fully open, everything becomes clearer and into focus. I see Chloe stood over me, her eyes bloodshot and her cheeks damp with tears. Mum and Dad are next to her. Mum is crying and Dad is in shock. The doctors are all fussing around me so they get pushed back, but Chloe stands firm at my side. She gazes down at me. "You're actually awake! You came back!" She cries, "I thought I was going to lose you. I was so scared, Chase. But you did it! You finally woke up!" I crack a small smile.
"O-o-o-of…course…I…d-did…" I croak, "I…c-c-c-couldn't..l-leave…you…" Chloe leans down and hugs me, crying into my shoulder and I slowly lift my arm and drape it around her. "I missed you so much! It hasn't been the same without you. Me without you is like living without air. I don't know what I would have done if I lost you!" I chuckle softly, wheezing a little. "W-we… go…t-together. T-two…o-of….a…k-kind…" Chloe stares at me and laughs lightly. "Yeah! We do! Like Bacon and Eggs! Or…" "F-fish…and…C-chips!" I add. Chloe giggles. "Exactly! Cause we're twins right."

I give her a wide grin. "Twins…forever!"

The End.

THE BUNKER

Hope: The Eternal Survivor

Drip. Drip. Drip.

The sound of tiny drops of water ripples through the dark hallowing room with a chilling echo. Shallow breaths shivering in the cold. They knew not of the time that had passed. Nor did they know what remained of the world they once knew. The innocent few survivors of a cold and cruel war.

Throughout the unknown days that have passed, not a moment creeps by without the ringing of explosions and people screaming in their ears. A reminder of the tragedy that occurred. Flashes from the trauma of something so cruel, if it weren't for having each other, many more may be lost. Life, so different in the dark sanctuary. Far from the same as how the world was once before. Time becoming almost a myth as the shell-shocked survivors stay patiently holding on for a sign. A sign of change. A sign of hope. Longing to return to the outside world. But not the old world. A new world. A world where they can thrive instead of just survive.

But none of them, not one, has forgotten. How could anyone forget? Forget the catastrophic tragedy. Or the harsh, brutal life in the world there once was.

The world once before was cold and wicked. Violence and Evil reigned their vile terror. Selfishness and greed prevailed. They held so much power, the very earth weakened to its knees. They cared not about who would be sacrificed, nor how it would affect the world. They knew not of kindness or peace, only hate and anger ran through their veins. They did not care for one another, believing in purely all for one and zilch for anyone else.

The world was a corrupt, wicked poison. Trying to trap a sliver of light in a raging web of darkness and smothering it in a choking venom. It was not long before the cauldron became so full of evil it began to overflow in a ferocious flood of chaos.

It started as one side against another but then the whole world started wanting a taste. Enter a mass wave of chaos and destruction. Of poverty and suffering. Millions of lives lost to this vile corruption by the hands of merciless villains.

But not all was lost. There were those who sensed it coming. Those who still believed in hope and love. Not knowing when, nor how much time remained for this cruel society, they set out fearlessly. Bunkers, 10 feet down and filled with supplies, were formed around the world. Next, a mission to warn and save as many as possible. A scurry of panic and fear. An urgency of survival. Thousands upon thousands fled to these shelters. Even the last few, that scrambled desperately as explosions tore through the earth and buildings fell to their demise, managed to clamber through. Falling into the arms of other survivors who pulled them to safety.

Bang!

Sealed in and finally safe. The bunkers closed tightly, protecting all those inside. Where they waited. And waited. And waited. For they knew there would be a time for them to return. Finally, that time has arrived.

With a creak and a clang, the old metal doors slowly open. Light floods in blinding everyone in sight. Then the survivors pour out. Walking, wandering, staring at what has remained. The world was silenced, rubble being the only survivor. Selfishness, hate, anger and greed all wiped themselves out along with the rest of the world.

A small silence to take in the surroundings. The rubble and dirt beneath their feet. The blue sky without a cloud in sight and the warm sun beaming down on them. They're alive. Ready to rebuild and live life again. This time to the fullest.

A second silence follows. A global mourning. Not for what once was. But for those who did not make it. For those who will not get to witness the rebirth of the world. For the loved ones lost. Lost to a mass devastation, but never once, not for a second, ever forgotten.

But then a glimmer, a flicker, a glow of golden light. A locket, with a heart shaped of gold, resting on the ashes of the world that once was. As it is picked up by the soft innocent hand of a child, it clicks open.

Within the heart of gold, a photo of a family. A family that survived. A reminder of how we are all one big family, all of us in this together. A reminder of hope, of how working together helps us all survive. How time and peace help a world rebuild from ruins. And how kindness and love help a fallen society to thrive.

PART FOUR

CHAPTER 18

EPILOGUE

by Pete

It is with great sadness that I have to write an ending to Lorna's book.

On Saturday 11th December 2019 Lorna and I celebrated our ninth Wedding Anniversary, Lorna surprised me by having bought tickets for a guided tour and tasting at the National Brewery Museum(formerly the Bass Museum) at Burton On Trent(I used to be a member of CAMRA - Campaign For Real Ale). We made a short weekend of it and stayed overnight in a nearby hotel, and slept in a four-poster bed - which added to the romance.

Everything seemed to be going so well. Earlier in the year, I had surprised Lorna by booking a holiday in Scarborough with tickets to a Cliff Richard concert (Lorna was a fan). In September 2019 we went to Bournemouth, and particularly enjoyed a show - That'll Be The Day, and the Sealife centre (Lorna really loved animals especially penguins), I didn't enjoy tripping up and falling flat on my face - I had two paramedics in attendance, one of whom glued my eyebrow back together.

In October I attended a Tribunal and was awarded PIPS (Personal Independence Payments) and with the back pay I was able to pay off all our debts. We had been struggling financially for years, at different times I was forced by circumstance to sell my grandfathers' First World War medals, and my wedding ring. As well as the PIPS award I was due to receive my State Pension on 6 January 2020, when that day came I thought we had got it made.

On Christmas Eve we both came down with a virus - sore throat, temperature and feeling woozy. By January 5th my symptoms had gone but Lorna's glands were still up, she had also been back to the dentist three times in as many months for pain in her mouth.

So on Monday, January 6th (the day when everything was going to be alright), we saw Lorna's GP. She had a feel around Lorna's lower jaw and neck, and told us she thought it was mumps and that we needed to self isolate for ten days, but that the swelling could last for up to three weeks. One of the lumps in Lorna's neck was more solid than the others and the doctor thought it could be a stone in the lymphatic system.

After two more visits to the GP and two appointments with the Consultant at Leicester Royal Infirmary, Lorna attended 6 outpatient appointments in 10 days - MRI scan, CT scan, blood tests, Xray of the jaw, ECG and thorough heart examination, lung capacity test and consultation with a consultant anaesthetist who told us that because Lorna hadn't been able to eat properly her red blood cell count was low.

At the very end of February, we went to see the Consultant who informed us that Lorna had primary tongue cancer, and secondary tumours in her mouth and neck. With the test results and reports from other consultants, he told us he was 100% certain he could get rid of it all - in four minor operations done at the same time - which then became a major eight-hour operation including a skin graft. She would be four or five days in intensive care and a further five days in hospital. Of course, an eight-hour operation could not be arranged straight away - we would have to wait for an appointment

Lorna received a letter to come in and see the Consultant on 17th March - we both thought Lorna was going to be given a date for the operation, which of course got our hopes up. When we got there the Consultant said the Covid epidemic was rampant in Leicester, and it was too big a risk to stay in hospital for ten days. He was going to have to refer Lorna to Oncology for Chemotherapy or Radiotherapy or both. We were both shocked, Lorna took it on the chin, I didn't say anything to Lorna but I was now scared.

Even by this time, Lorna was having difficulty swallowing, I bought a blender to puree food, but Lorna was relying more and more on Fortisip(a yoghurt type drink of different flavours mainly fruit) and Complan. She was also in pain and was prescribed combinations of painkillers and morphine. It was almost a daily ritual for me to be in touch with the hospital, GP or Pharmacy to ensure that we had sufficient Fortisip and medication, each party had a slightly different idea as to who did what and when, the Macmillan nurses were there for support and put us in touch with the right people. "The hospital" included Oncology, a Dietitian who was trying to increase Lorna's weight, and when Lorna had a RIG(peg) fitted a specialist for that.

For the last few years Lorna had mobility problems, and had used a mobility scooter to get out and about, and also had a carer in each morning to help her shower and dress, because of Covid, that was the only visitor we usually had. So that just left the two of us to cope and carry on.

After several weeks, Lorna received an appointment to see a Consultant Oncologist, because of Covid I had to sit in the outer waiting room, after three hours Lorna returned and told me she was starting a five-day course of radiotherapy the next week. Before that Lorna was to have a RIG fitted - a narrow tube that fed into her stomach, and by using a syringe pushing food etc. through. Lorna now had to have all water, food and medication through the tube. All water used had to be boiled first then allowed to cool, and all the syringes had to be thoroughly cleaned in hot soapy water. I usually administered the syringe, morning, noon and night, if Lorna was in pain in the middle of the night I might have to administer morphine. So neither of us was getting anything like the right amount of sleep. Also when I was using the syringe, I was sitting next to her and stretching across, it didn't bother me at the time but I badly strained my left hamstring - and it still bothers me over a year later. Also, we had a District Nurse once a week to change the water in the balloon that was attached to the tube in Lorna's stomach, and to clean and redress the wound. I used to clean and dress the wound at least once a day.

Lorna had the first five days of radiotherapy treatment in the middle of May and the Oncologist recommended a break and then a further 15 or 25 treatments starting on 29 June.

At teatime on Monday 15th of June Lorna started bleeding from the mouth - which stopped just before the paramedics arrived, they checked her over and checked with the hospital who told us if there was any more bleeding to ring first thing the next morning. The paramedics said if the bleeding returned and got worse to call them back. Lorna had some smaller bleeds overnight, so first thing we rang the Macmillan nurse, who asked us to come in that morning to see the original Maxillofacial Consultant. They kept her in overnight and used medicines, mouthwash and a spray to stop the bleeding. They also brought her next sessions of Radiotherapy to Monday 22nd of June.

By this time we had been given a machine to pump Lorna's main meal into her tummy overnight - it took 7 hours. So Monday 22nd we were up at 6am to flush her overnight feed through, take her medications and water, to be ready for the carer who was calling at seven to help her wash and dress. The ambulance car could arrive to take Lorna to hospital anytime from 7.45, it was usually around 9am - if so Lorna had time to have a feed, and to have more water.

Everything went OK on the Monday, apart from Lorna mentioning that the only other passenger in the ambulance car had been coughing a lot, but both passengers and the driver were wearing masks. On the Tuesday, they put Lorna on the day ward for a while as she'd had trouble breathing, and diagnosed an infection, and Lorna returned home later with two bottles of liquid penicillin to take through the tube. I did notice Lorna was finding it hard to breathe, and also to use her sleep apnoea breathing mask. When all the radiotherapy was completed we were planning a five day coach holiday in the Lake District which we were both very much looking forward to, having been virtual prisoners in our own home since Christmas Eve. Lorna went to Radiotherapy on Wednesday and Thursday and was seen by the medical staff there.

Lorna was obviously not too well, but got up at 6am on Friday morning, the ambulance car arrived at 8.45 and I carried Lorna's heavy craft bag to the car for her, while Lorna carried her handbag, I kissed her goodbye as always.

At 10.30 I got a call saying that they were concerned about Lorna's breathing and that they were keeping her in for a day or two to help sort her breathing out. They would ring me later to let me know what ward she was on so I could take her things and her sleep mask and machine in.

A little later at 12.15, I got a call from the hospital to come in at once, so I asked about bringing in Lorna's things, the sister said that she didn't think that they would be needed. I said "Is it that bad" the sister told me that Lorna had crashed and she was being worked on as we spoke. I shot off by taxi wondering what I would find when I got there and fearing the worst might have already happened. I thought about asking other people in - but it might have already been too late.

When I got there they kept me waiting for a quarter of an hour, and told me that Lorna was very poorly, and they could do little for her - and the outcome didn't look good. Because of the size of the tumours, they couldn't insert a tube down her throat to help her breathe nor perform a tracheotomy. All they could do was give her a little oxygen and some medication to help her breathe. When I was allowed in the room, Lorna's eyes were open but she didn't look conscious. She came round a bit and kept calling on Jehovah to help her. She also kept saying Tim(one of the Elders from the Kingdom Hall) so I asked if she wanted Tim to come in, and Lorna nodded. I asked Lorna if she wanted her daughter Lydia to come in as well and she nodded again, so a nurse went off to give them both a ring. I texted Lorna's mother Maureen to let her know what was happening, I didn't know what to do about her father Roy who is very deaf and doesn't have a mobile, that was about 1.45pm. A bit later Lydia and her stepmother arrived and Tim, I put them in the picture, and let Tim sit next to Lorna and he gave her a few bible readings and said a prayer, then Tim left and went to get Lorna's father Roy.

Lydia was holding one of Lorna's hands, and I was holding the other and kept telling her I loved her and rubbed her shoulder, I told her that Lydia was there and Lorna nodded. Lydia's father John replaced her stepmother. Over the next hour or so Lorna's breathing became shallower so I called a nurse, she said that Lorna wasn't getting much oxygen now and her extremities - feet and arms were getting cold as they were closing down. She gave Lorna an injection to help her breathe, John and I left for a while so Lydia could have some private time. The nurse told us that Lorna might breathe just once a minute. Tim arrived with Roy and I let them sit next to Lorna, at that moment I hadn't seen Lorna breathe for a while, I thought I felt a faint pulse and went to get someone. The doctor and nurse asked us all to leave, and came out a few minutes later to tell us that Lorna had gone, it was a quarter to five. Lorna was 49 years old.

It was absolutely the worst day in my entire life.

We were all stunned, Roy and I went back in to sit with Lorna, after a while Roy left the room and everyone else made their way home. I sat with Lorna for twenty minutes, kissed her goodbye, and collected her belongings, picked up some information on what happens next which proved to be very useful over the next few days. I rang Lorna's sister in Scotland who was going to ring her mum, and her other sister in London.

Lorna and I had discussed what we both wanted in the way of funerals and Lorna told me she wanted a burial. The Friday before the funeral I went to see Lorna in an open coffin, I broke down for a while, I'd asked that Lorna be buried wearing her new blue dress which she had recently bought because she had lost so much weight during her illness. Lorna was into reborn baby dolls who she doted on, the first was Lulu and the second was Jacob - I placed a woolen hat from each in the coffin, also our ninth Wedding Anniversary cards to each other, and the Cliff Richard T-shirt I'd bought for her earlier in the year, I'd wanted to include a photograph of her daughter Lydia but unfortunately I couldn't find one.

For the funeral, Covid regulations were still in force and on the day I'd visited Lorna they changed from allowing eight people at the funeral to twenty people. Also on that day travel restrictions in Scotland were lifted enabling Lorna's sister and her husband to come down for the funeral.

I have to say that I thought that I knew Lorna before the cancer, I thought that she would find it all too much, but I didn't know her - apart from a couple of days when she was fed up, and an odd few minutes she took it all on her chin and just got on with it. She was the bravest person that I've ever known. As well as our holiday in the Lake District Lorna was looking forward to her craft work - book folding, crochet and knitting. She was so positive "I'm going to fight this to the very end, I'm not going to let this beat me," she said practically every day.

I'd been having a bad time with bereavements - in September 2019 my elder brother John had died suddenly, in December my oldest friend's wife passed away suddenly, then came Lorna's illness and passing, and less than two months later my eldest niece Alison passed away suddenly at the age of 47.

There are a lot of "If Onlys" - if only someone had picked up on Lorna losing a stone in weight in November and another stone in December 2019. If only someone could have found the cancer under Lorna's tongue earlier. If only the hospital appointment had been earlier(we did have an appointment with the Consultant cancelled on the day and weren't able to see him for another ten days). If only the Covid outbreak had happened a few weeks later. If only Lorna's Radiotherapy had started earlier. If only Lorna hadn't picked up an infection. If only Lorna had been given a stronger dose of penicillin.

None of that is of any use of course. For the first six months after Lorna's death, it felt like I was expecting her to come home sometime. In the New Year 2021, I accepted that this wasn't going to happen. I miss Lorna all the time, I have little conversations with her. I don't think that I will ever get over her death, there's an empty space in our bed where Lorna is supposed to be, and an empty space in my life as well. I had Lorna's grave dug to a double depth so my ashes can be placed there when my time comes.

Bereavement is hell, the only comforts that I have are that my darling Lorna was spared a long and painful illness, and that she had an absolute belief in her faith and in the resurrection.

This is a poem that that was read out at Lorna's funeral:

It's hard to know just what to say
When the one we love has passed away. And the life that we once shared so bright, now feels empty, cold, like the darkest night.

Lorna was much loved and touched all our lives, as a daughter, sister, mother and wife.
And although we may grieve in our different ways,
the love we all share for her will always be in our hearts unitedly.

Draw comfort in knowing that,
the pain and suffering that is now so strong will one day soon all be gone.

It was Lorna's faith and hope that helped her cope, And she was so strong.
She believed she will live again. And God will not prove her wrong!

So when she wakes up from her sleep and rest,
and is feeling at her very best and life as good as it can be, What will Lorna want to see?
That's easy.
She will want to be surrounded by all her family.

EPILOGUE (CONTINUED)

by Lydia

When this book was started, I never imagined having to write something like this. I never imagined anything like this could happen.

December 2019, Mum was quite ill. Both she and Pete caught a virus around Christmas time. Pete started feeling better but mum didn't and because she was ill, I was unable to go down and see her on the weekends as I'd normally do. It quickly rolled over to 2020 and I'd only been able to see her once, due to her illness. But we stayed in touch over Facebook.

And as we know, in early 2020, the world was hit by a pandemic which in turn caused a lot of chaos and grief for many people. In March 2020, when I was returning home from spending my morning at the animal shelter where I volunteer, I received a message from my Mum. A message that pretty much changed my life. *'I've had test results from the hospital and I'm sorry I have some bad news. I have just found out that I have got cancer.'*

Looking back on that day, I remember the shock and the fear. The first place my mind went to was that I might lose my mum. My Dad wasn't happy that she'd texted it and thought it would have been better by a phone call. Which is true, but I can imagine how scared and distraught she'd have been. And how do you tell someone you have cancer? How do you get the words out? How do you even come to terms with something like that? And how do you respond to something like that?

I had no clue what to say back or how to process it all and it took me a week before I was able to reply. I knew she had been sick for a while, which is why I hadn't been able to see her for quite some time. But I never imagined it could be something this bad. And the pandemic put visiting her on hold for a long time. Throughout everything, I badly wanted to see her. I missed her incredibly and I know she wanted me there more than anything, but I couldn't risk her health with everything that was happening at the time.

Sometimes I wish I could've done more, like stay in touch more, I don't think I talked to her enough. She would message me all the time. Sometimes updates, sometimes encouraging words. It always amazed me how strong she was through all of it and how much she fought through it. There were a few times she had a few short stays in hospital and she would phone me from there and we'd chat, though it was always a struggle for her as the cancer was in her tongue (and later her throat), which affected her speech and her ability to eat.

Mum was supposed to have surgery but due to the pandemic, she was unable to have it. Maybe if she did she'd still be here, or at least had a bit more time. But I guess we'll never know.

As we started to come out of the first lockdown, Mum and I began to make plans. Finally, we arranged for me to go over to her house and we'd sit in the garden. We'd chat and catch up, play some music, sing, and even play a few games. The 27th of June was going to be a great day! Unfortunately, though, a day before we were supposed to meet, our plans were put on hold.

Friday 26th June 2020, mum went into hospital for a routine hospital appointment. Later that morning, I got a message from Pete saying that mum would be kept in overnight and that it wouldn't be possible for us to meet up the following day as planned. I didn't think too much of it, just hoping that mum was doing okay and that we'll arrange to meet another time. However around 1-2 pm that afternoon, I got a call from the hospital from the Macmillan nurse. Straight away I had this feeling in the pit of my stomach, I just knew it was bad. Then I was told to come into the hospital as soon as I could because mum was really poorly. I knew there and then that I was going to lose my mum but every part of me tried to force it into the back of my mind, thinking that it was just me being my typical paranoid self. That it was just my anxiety talking.

But my gut instincts have never been wrong and the one time I wanted them to be, they were spot on.

I remember the next events vividly. Heading to the hospital with both Dad and my stepmom accompanying me, arriving at the ward and being led to her room. It took me a few minutes to compose myself as I was already very upset before even going into the room. When I walked into that room and saw Pete's face, it all hit me like a truck. My mum was dying. My worst fears were coming true.

That day replays in my mind constantly like a stuck record. The conversations I had with Pete and both of us staying by mum's bedside. Which I know she would've wanted. A member of the hospital liaison committee and from her congregation in the Jehovah's Witnesses came and said a prayer for us. He also brought my grandad to the hospital so he could say his goodbyes but that was a bit later on.

I had heard from Pete how she had to be resuscitated earlier in the day which really shook me. But now I believe that mum held on so I could be there in time. We were in the room for at least a few hours and the whole time mum was mostly unconscious. There was one point when she came round but she wasn't fully aware of things. She came round a second time and she was more aware. Pete spoke to her and told her I was here. I moved so she could see me. It was not long after that, that she started to go. But the whole time I was in the room, I kept praying and praying for a miracle, that she would be saved, even though I knew it was hopeless.

I'm not sure at what point she passed, but Dad and Pete left the room a bit later on, to give me some time with her because we knew she was going to go very very soon. So I talked to her. I said all the things I needed to say. All the things I wanted her to know. The most important of all was how much I loved her and that she was the best mum in the world. A while later Pete noticed she hadn't taken a breath for a while and got a doctor. When they came, we were told to leave the room, so we did. A few minutes later they emerged from her room and told us the devastating news that she was gone. It felt like my whole world had come crashing down and I began sobbing uncontrollably.

When I got home that day, I had to make a difficult phone call to mum's best friend Tammy (Who also happens to be my best friend's mum.) to let her know what had happened. That was the hardest phone call I've ever had to make.

Losing her was by far the hardest thing I've ever had to go through. I miss her incredibly and not a day goes by when I don't think of her. I'm always looking at old photos, old message conversations and old videos. I've felt so numb throughout this whole thing, it's like my mind and emotions just shut down - until it became too much and caused me to have multiple breakdowns. I never imagined I'd be without her. It saddens me that she won't be there when I eventually find love and get married. Or when I have children. She's always wanted to be a grandma but she'll never get to meet them. I'll tell them about her though and show them the memory book I've been making.

Not a day goes by when she doesn't appear in my thoughts. And while that day still haunts me and probably always will, I keep my focus on all the wonderful memories I have with her, all the things we used to do together. My favourite memories are when we've been to concerts together. There is a special duo that holds such a place in my heart as their music has helped me through so many of the things I've been through. They're called Bars and Melody and were on Britain's

Got Talent in 2014. You may have heard of their song Hopeful. I've been a fan of them since their audition and I got my mum hooked on them as well. I sometimes think she may have been an even bigger fan than me. She always used to go to the concerts with me (We pretty much always had VIP tickets, so we got to meet them) and we always had the best times. Mum always used to do some funny things.

The first time we met them was at a signing in 2015 for their single 'Stay Strong' and the first thing she did when we saw them was scream at them. At one point she also took her top off in front of them (It was their merch and she also had a second t shirt on underneath – thankfully, otherwise that would have been very awkward.) and demanded they sign it. There was also the time she announced she needed 'A pee' in front of them. At the time, both of these situations were so embarrassing, but now, I look back on them with a fond smile. At the concerts she'd be singing loudly and proudly above everyone else, having the time of her life. We used to get stares, whispers, giggles, and nasty comments because she was in a wheelchair and because of her size.

But she never cared what anyone thought of her. She just kept being her loud, bubbly self. And of course teased me constantly about one particular member of the duo that I may or may not have a crush on. The two guys from Bars and Melody are called Charlie and Leo, (but I'm not telling you which one I have a crush on. Haha!) and their kindness to us at these shows made the experience even more amazing.

I remember all the times we used to bake, cook, go shopping together, play games and best of all…sing! We both loved to have karaoke sessions, singing at the top of our lungs. We'd always used to have a good laugh together. She'd also be there for me throughout all the bad times I went through and she supported me through my struggles with mental health. Mum understood the struggles better than anyone else I know and understood me the most as well. She would always be there to give me a cuddle when I needed it and comfort me when I cried, reassuring me.

I miss her so much. I miss all of the good times and the craziest thing is, I even miss the bad. There were times when we didn't get on. We could be like chalk and cheese at times. We had quite a few arguments, some worse than others (we sometimes went weeks without seeing each other afterwards. One time it was even a few months) but we always made up. I never stopped loving her and I know she loved me too. Mum never failed to remind me just how much I meant to her. To me, she's the best mum in the world and I wish I had told her that more because she didn't always believe it and sometimes thought she'd let me down.

Mum, you never did let me down. Not even once. And although we had our ups and downs, I couldn't ask for a better mum. You're the best mum in the world, because you were MY mum! There's a huge hole in my heart now you're gone and I don't know if I'll ever be the same. But although you're no longer with us physically, you'll always live on in our hearts and through all the memories we shared with you.

I love you mum. xx

ABOUT THE AUTHOR

Lorna was born in Leicestershire, United Kingdom, in 1971, she loved life and people. From her first marriage she had her only child, a daughter Lydia. Lorna was diagnosed with Bipolar Disorder in 2000, and had several hospital stays, during which she wrote her first book "Snappy But Happy" a self help book on Mental Health Issues.

Lorna might have described herself as an "ordinary" person - but she actually proved to be Extraordinary. She faced whatever life threw at her with courage and positivity. She just got on with it, whether it was Bipolar Disorder, insulin dependent diabetes, sleep apnoea and finally cancer. She wrote her second book (this one) but sadly passed away in 2020 before it could be published. As most of her Consultants' letters say "she was a lovely Lady" as you can see for yourself.

Printed in the United States
by Baker & Taylor Publisher Services